Nomvuyo Ngcelwane

SALA KAHLE,
DISTRICT SIX

An African Woman's Perspective

KWELA BOOKS

The author wishes to express her sincere gratitude
to the following people for granting her permission to
reproduce their photographs in this book:
Olive Cele, Albert Makabane
Nomathemba Mketo, Jeanette Ncapai
Elizabeth Njobe, Nomsa Qila
Ronnie Mogorosi, Rueben Mdlalo
and Connie Siboto

The photograph on the front cover also appears on p. 53; the
photograph on the title page is of a young Mrs Nokhubeka
and baby Mbijana of William Street – also pictured on p. 13.

Cover design and typography by Nazli Jacobs
Set in New Century Schoolbook
Printed and bound by National Book Printers
Drukkery Street, Goodwood, Western Cape
First edition, first printing 1998

ISBN 0-7957-0081-4

ACKNOWLEDGEMENTS

I would like to thank the members of my family for coaxing me into writing this book, especially Sonwabo Ngcelwane, Layton Ngcelwane and Benjamin Malobola. Their comments and questions have proved most valuable in presenting what should be known about the lives of African residents of District Six.

I would also like to express my sincerest gratitude to Thandi Makupula, Cyril Mandindi, Zolisa Gcilishe and Season Mdlalo for the important information we shared, and my publisher Annari van der Merwe, who also edited the manuscript.

This book is dedicated to all the families of District Six who were forcibly removed due to the implementation of the Group Areas Act of 1950.

CONTENTS

1

PENNY FOR YOUR THOUGHTS

"Penny for your thoughts?" said my brother one Sunday afternoon in March 1996. He had just been telling me about a meeting he had attended on behalf of the family in one of the primary schools in Guguletu. Word had gone round the Cape Town townships, as well as on television, that like the other groupings, African people who were forcibly removed from District Six during the 1960s due to the implementation of the Group Areas Act also qualified for compensation from the government.

"This move is surprising, dear brother," I said, "really surprising, since it is seldom if ever acknowledged that Africans, too, used to live in District Six. People only know of the experiences of their former Coloured neighbours."

I stood up and looked out of the window of his house at NY 75 No. 7 Guguletu, the four-roomed house to which my parents were forcibly removed in 1963.

"I sound racist, don't I?" I said. "But I'm not. It's just that it is often forgotten that we hold the same sentiments about the place as them. Don't we? How on earth can I be expected to forget twenty years of my life? That's ridiculous!"

Ideas were beginning to creep into my head. A few days before, I had seen on television a District Six museum which I was not aware of. I had looked it up in the telephone directory and had discovered that it was at 25a Buitenkant Street. I knew the place all right. I picked up the telephone and started dialling. The reply came from an answering machine. All I had wanted to know was their opening and closing times so that I might make time to go there one afternoon and say hello.

I was brought back to reality by my brother asking, "Do you want to do something about it?"

The urgency in his voice pulled me down in my chair. I looked at him and smiled. "Yes, of course, I'm thinking of doing something about it."

I returned to my place later that afternoon. After supper, I took a pen and paper and started writing the names of the streets I still remembered:

Cross	Mount
Richmond	Primrose
Arundel	Longmarket
Ashley	Wicht
Stone	De Villiers
Roos	Tennant
Frere	McKenzie
Constitution	Aspeling
Stuckeris	Rutger
Roger	Selkirk
Chapel	Russel
Reform	Horstley

"Not bad, lady, not bad," I said to myself, looking at the growing list.

HOME

I grew up at No. 22 Cross Street in District Six, the third child in a family of four, my only brother, Layton, being the youngest.

Cross Street ran parallel to Ashley Street, where the white Moravian church with the green roof is still standing today. But the area around the church building is now strewn with heaps of stones, the remains of what must have been people's homes then. The only visible reminder of District Six is the few streets that still carry their old names. The church building has been incorporated into the Cape Technikon and is now used as a keep-fit gym by the students.

I was brought to this earth by midwives from the Peninsula Maternity Hospital just a few hundred yards away, at the corner of Caledon and Mount Streets. The building is still there although the facilities were moved to Mowbray years ago.

My father, I was told, wanted a son because he already had two daughters, Nombulelo and Nompumelelo, but when he was shown the new baby who resembled his favourite sister so much, he named me Nomvuyo – "to rejoice" – and loved me as much as he would have loved a son.

When I was five days old I was taken to No. 22 Cross Street where my parents rented a room in a double-storey building owned by Abdullah. They paid eleven shillings (when the old British money system was decimalised in 1961 it was the equivalent of one rand and ten cents) for rent, and this was collected by the landlord on the first Saturday of each month.

Everybody would be on the lookout for Abdullah on this Saturday. Those who had to be away left their rents with their neighbours to hand over to him. What was amazing about this landlord was that he never had any problem in writing down the surnames of his Black tenants and that he knew each and every tenant in the building.

"Morning, tata, morning, mama, and morning to you, boy and girls," he would greet us, announcing himself and waiting at the door until he was allowed in. We all knew that he had to be offered a chair at the table so that he could write out the receipt.

"Fine weather today, neh, tata?" he would remark on the condition of the weather each time, while writing out the receipt.

If my parents were going to be away they would leave the rent with my eldest sister, Nombulelo, or Thelma, as she was also known. Abdullah knew this arrangement and on such days, after greeting us, he would ask, "Is there something for me today?"

"Yes, sir," my sister would reply, offering him a chair and then taking out the money which my father always gave in the form of a ten-shilling note and a one-shilling coin.

Abdullah was a very polite man who treated his tenants well, and unusually prompt in attending to their complaints. His building was well maintained, much better than most of the other buildings in the area. Our room was upstairs. We had to climb a flight of thirteen steps to get there. It had a beautiful view. From the windows one could see the yellow Muir Street Zainatul Mosque, the Foreshore and Table Bay. There was enough light and it was very cosy in winter.

Our room was the biggest room upstairs. It had two windows, both facing north. As you entered, immediately on the left were two chairs for visitors. At the left end were two beds with two mattresses each, separated by a wardrobe. One bed was for my parents and the other for my two sisters. My brother and I slept on a mattress on the floor.

In front of the beds were two identical floor rugs and my father's armchair stood in front of the wardrobe. These two beds were my mother's pride. She took great care in making them up and they were always covered in identical bedspreads, which made them look like twin beds. Her favourite type of bedspread was made of "candlewick" and she had three sets – pink, white and lemon. The colours usually matched her curtaining.

In the middle of the room stood a dining table with four chairs. Between the two windows was a sideboard with ornaments on top. My mother got these from the White families she charred for. All our dishes were kept inside the sideboard. In the right-hand corner stood a cupboard with shelves covered in newspaper with beautiful cut-out designs which my mother did herself. This is where her dinner set was displayed.

Next to the cupboard was an oilcloth-covered table with two stoves – a primus and a Beatrice – as well as a bucket with water which we used for washing dishes and for drinking, because the tap was downstairs. This water bucket was always covered with a tray. Pots and two big bowls for washing dishes were kept under this table.

My mother did charwork three times a week – on Mondays, Wednesdays and Fridays. On these days we knew where to get the key. It was left with Malikwe, one of the residents who was a full-time housewife. When we got inside the room, the first thing we did was to take off our school uniform and put on play clothes, before having lunch, which was

Albert and Mamiya Makhabane lived at No. 26 Cross Street. Here they are with a nephew and niece visiting from the country. Having formal photographs taken was very popular at the time.

usually leftovers of the previous evening's supper. Nombulelo would warm them for us, and after lunch we did our homework.

My mother came back from her char jobs round about four o'clock. We used to time her and on her approach, Layton and I would run downstairs to meet her and help her with her bag. On her arrival, Nombulelo had to make tea for her. My mother would throw herself on the chair, breathing heavily, then take off her shoes and relax.

"What have you brought us today, Mama?" Layton would ask. She would not answer directly, but would first enjoy her tea before saying, "Pass me my bag." She would then take out her parcels which always included something for us, either fruit or buns, or sweets. With broad smiles we would individually say, *"Enkosi,* Mama," accepting the gift with both hands.

Mrs Nokhubeka, who lived in William Street, with her sons Mbijana and Mnyamezeli. Unlike most other Black families in District Six, the Nokhubekas could afford all kinds of luxuries – like fancy clothes.

Olive, the daughter of Mrs Nokhubeka of William Street, and her husband Michael Cele on their way to visit friends in BoKaap, in 1955. BoKaap, like District Six, had many Black residents at the time.

My father came back from his work at the United Tobacco Company in Observatory at about half past five with his lunch-box, a tin box with a handle, in one hand and his newspaper under his arm. Layton was the only one who met my father and he would be rewarded with a sandwich which my father always kept for him.

My father had a queer way of greeting, saying, "Watchie," which always brought a smile to my mother's face. Nombulelo had to make tea for him as well. After tea, my father would go downstairs to wash in a tub in the backyard. After that, he would sit in his armchair and read his paper until suppertime. We all sat at the table to eat.

After supper, my sisters tidied the table and washed the dishes. We then sat for a while and talked to our parents about school, bragging about the marks we got. Sometimes we recited new poems or helped each other in memorising them. Both our parents were encouraging and did not allow us to fall behind.

We would then be called upon by my father to say the Lord's Prayer and our parents took turns in praying. This was our weekdays routine.

Cross Street was not very long. It was blocked off at both ends: at one end, by a blank wall, and at the other, by a small church hall which we called the Mission. From one end to the other you could see all the way.

You could enter our street either from Richmond or from Arundel Street, which ran between Hanover and Constitution Street.

Our building, with its four front doors, stood at the same end as the Mission. Each door led to three rooms downstairs and two upstairs. The whole building, from No. 22 to No. 28, was occupied by Black tenants.

It was quite unusual that most of us shared the same clan name: ama-Bhele. The surnames were Bhenya, Mabandla, Makhabane, Makupula, Mpazi, Ngcelwane, Njobe and Ntshiba, but according to our Xhosa culture, the men were all brothers by virtue of having the same clan name, and this was how they treated each other. The other family groups who stayed in our building did not belong to the Mbele clan, but still they were treated with love and respect.

There was no doubt that all these people were Christians and that their motto was "Love thy neighbour".

Like ours, the four other rooms at No. 22 were occupied by one family to a room. There was a communal kitchen, and it was in this kitchen that the families met to formulate rules for the group of tenants. The families shared the same washing line, the same outside toilet, one rubbish bin and one postbox. It was therefore necessary for the group to draw up some rules so as to avoid friction and conflict. The rules stated very plainly the days on which each family had to clean the toilet, take out the rubbish bin, open the letterbox and hand over the mail to the relevant people, could use the washing line, and so forth. This resulted in perfect harmony and tolerance.

GOING TO SCHOOL IN DISTRICT SIX

My family worshipped at the Methodist church in Chapel Street. The church had a hall which was used as a junior primary school, the only school for Black children in District Six. It was a one-room, two-teacher school. A woman taught Sub A and Sub B, as the first two years of school were then known, and a male teacher, who also used to be the principal, was responsible for the next two years, Stds 1 and 2. The two class groups were separated by a partition.

Most of the children knew the school environment before they even started school, because the church hall was used for Sunday school as well, which most of us attended. I even knew where my sister, Nompumelelo, sat in her Sub B class. By the time we started school at six years, we knew more or less what to expect.

I was so eager for this day to come, little expecting it to start on a bad note. Nompumelelo, who was going to be in the Std 1 class that year, was asked to register me. My mother wrote down all the details on a writing pad page which she put in an envelope. I did not have any problem with that, but what I could not accept was the fact that I had to take Nompumelelo's old slate for writing. She was going to use exercise books in her next class. Books and stationery at the time were bought by our parents and not by the school.

"No, Mama, I'm not going to use Nompumelelo's slate! I want my own," I said, refusing to take the slate which Nompumelelo was offering me.

"Don't be silly, Nomvuyo," my mother scolded. "I can't buy a new slate when we still have this one." She took the slate from Nompumelelo and showed it to me.

"Look, it is still in a good condition, Nomvuyo," she said, trying to convince me, but I looked away. That I suppose made her angry.

"Take it!" she screamed at me.

I put my hands behind my back, demonstrating that I was not going to take it.

She grabbed me by the arm and instructed Nompumelelo to bring her my father's belt. I tried to pull away but she held me tight. Nompumelelo went to the wardrobe, but she hesitated to open it. She turned around and said, "Please, Mama, forgive her."

"Nompumelelo!" my mother shouted. "Do you want me to spank you as well?"

My sister immediately opened the wardrobe, took out the belt and handed it to my mother, who did not waste time but held me up in the air and gave me a few strokes. I was still screaming, "Sorry, Mama, I won't do it again," when she pushed me away from her and handed me the slate, saying, "Take it!"

I took the slate and ran down the stairs.

I cried all the way down Hanover Street. Some of the passers-by who noticed enquired, "Doesn't she want to go to school?"

I do not think Nompumelelo said anything. All I can remember is that she was pulling me by my arm, walking very fast because we were late.

16

When we were at the corner of Muir and Chapel Streets she stopped, turned to me and said, *"Ukuba awuthuli, soze uthathwe esikolweni uzenz'usana nje!"* – If you do not stop crying, you won't be admitted to school because you're behaving like a baby.

I quickly dried my eyes and followed her. When we approached the gate, some of her friends came to join us. They were chatting about their new class. Nompumelelo excused herself and took me inside the hall where we found a group of parents with children of my age standing in a queue next to the principal's table to register. We joined the end of the queue. When our turn came, Nompumelelo greeted the principal and handed over the envelope my mother had given her.

The principal wrote down the particulars and instructed my sister to take me to Miss Thutha on the other side of the partition. On this side was a group of children of my age, boys and girls, sitting on desks. I knew some of them and when they saw me one of them whispered, *"Nanku uNomvuyo uza kufunda nathi."* – Here's Nomvuyo, she's going to be in our class.

"Why is she crying, Nompumelelo?" Miss Thutha asked. "Is she scared of school?"

"No, miss," replied Nompumelelo. "It's only that she doesn't want to use an old slate."

"Come, sisi, this slate is as good as new. Bring her a little water to drink, she's going to be okay," said Miss Thutha, hugging me and assuring me that I was going to be happy at school.

When the water arrived in a mug, I drank a little and Nompumelelo took me to my seat and told me that she would see me at breaktime. By the end of that first day, I was happy to be in Miss Thutha's class.

SCHOOL AND GAMES

It was school policy that every pupil had to attend Sunday school. Miss Thutha was also the Sunday school teacher. She kept a register of Sunday school attendance which she handed to Mr Kakaza, the principal, every Monday morning. Pupils who could not attend Sunday school had to bring written excuses from their parents.

"Ndakunibetha ezimpundwini kube nzima ukuhlala," – If you stay away from Sunday school without a good excuse, I'll spank you – Mr Kakaza warned us.

Most of the pupils obeyed this rule and it was usually not necessary for Mr Kakaza to use the cane on anybody. But one Monday morning when the list was given to him, it turned out that one of the big boys in Std 1, Winkie, had not attended. Winkie had brought a letter from his parents.

The principal read the letter and said nothing, but at the end of that day he asked one of the boys, Welcome, also in Std 1, to take a letter to Winkie's parents in Caledon Street.

The following day, Winkie's mother came to school. Because there was no principal's office at the school, Mr Kakaza met her at the door. We could not pick up what he was saying to her but we clearly heard Winkie's mother say, "It's not true, principal, I didn't send him anywhere on Sunday morning and my husband and I did not write you any letter."

Everybody was now gazing at Winkie who was clearly beginning to feel uneasy. Some of the boys were showing with their hands that he was going to get a good spanking. After his mother had left, the principal came back and called Winkie to his desk.

"Where were you on Sunday morning?" he demanded, looking very serious.

"I ..." started Winkie but the principal interrupted.

"Look, boy, I want the truth, do you hear me?"

"Yes, sir," replied Winkie with a trembling voice.

"Did your mother send you to Woodstock on Sunday morning, Winkie?"

Winkie kept quiet and started scratching his head.

The principal opened his cupboard, took out the letter and asked, "Who wrote this letter, Winkie?"

"It was another boy who goes to school at Langa."

"What's his name and which school does he attend?"

"I don't know the name of the school, sir, but his name is Willie-Boy."

"Whose idea was it, Winkie?"

"It was Willie-Boy's idea, sir."

"When you meet him again, you must tell him what you got from me," the principal said, taking off his jacket.

He asked four boys from Std 2 to bring a bench from the back of the hall. Winkie was instructed to lie down on the bench, and while the other boys held his arms and legs, he was given four good lashes with a thin cane.

Winkie twisted and turned and screamed until Mr Kakaza told the other boys to let him go. After that, the principal gave him a piece of foolscap paper and told him to write a full page of *SOZE NDIPHINDE NDIVUME UKUQHATHWA* – I SHALL NEVER ALLOW MYSELF TO BE MIS-LED AGAIN.

Winkie became very quiet and isolated after the incident. When we were in Std 2, he dropped out just before the mid-year exams and we never saw him again.

There was no playground at the Methodist church in Chapel Street, so we played on the streets. Our break was only fifteen minutes and the games we played varied. The girls would sometimes play hopscotch just behind the church hall in Laser Street, while the boys played football in front of the gate in Chapel Street, or sometimes round the corner in Muir Street. *Ikula* was also popular with girls. We would all stand in a circle, singing and clapping, with one girl in the middle. She would invite someone to come forward and they would hold hands and swing round. The first girl would then leave the middle to join the circle, while the newcomer would indicate to another girl to come forward and swing with her.

Because there was no bell, we were not allowed to play far from the school, as it would be difficult to call everybody back after break. This rule was never broken. Year after year, every pupil adhered to it.

When I was in Sub B, the principal announced during assembly one morning that a photographer had been organised to come to the school to take pictures of every pupil – for one shilling per photo. We were thrilled. Our parents were requested by letter to support the project, as a certain percentage of the money would be donated towards the school fund.

"Wear your Sunday best," Mr Kakaza suggested. "But be sure to put on our school blazer."

The money was collected by Miss Thutha before the photographer arrived, an Indian guy. As soon as he had set up his camera, we were told to stand in threes. There was a lot of excitement as pupils tried to find their friends and stand with them, while Miss Thutha was doing her best to arrange us her way.

Because there were more girls than boys, it was necessary that some of the groups be mixed, and the boys did not like this.

"We can't take photos with girls, miss," Sipho protested, pushing me aside.

"Sipho, why are you pushing? There's enough space for everybody," was Miss Thutha's response.

"No, miss, we don't want to stand with girls," Sipho insisted.

"There's nothing wrong with that. We're not taking group photos," Miss Thutha explained. "If you push again, I'll make you stand at the back and tell the photographer not to take your picture."

After that warning, there was order.

When the photographer was through with us lot, Mr Kakaza announced we would get our photos in two weeks. When they finally arrived and everybody received their photo, I carried mine home as if it was a piece of gold. It is still in our family album.

The total enrolment at the school was less than 150. Even the combined standards had a reasonable number of pupils and our teachers handled the classes well.

Our classroom was divided in two. On one side was Sub A, on the other, Sub B. Both groups had a blackboard which stood on an easel.

In the mornings, we shared the Scripture lesson, but after that we separated for Arithmetic. Our teacher was clever at alternating new lessons. If Sub A were going to be taught a new concept, Sub B would be given written work which they could do on their own, and vice versa. At first, we found it difficult when Miss Thutha was doing work that was not intended for us, but later on, we got used to her teaching method.

In Std 1 and Std 2 we wrote on slates. I didn't have to keep Nompumelelo's old slate for very long. These things broke nearly every week, and new ones had to be purchased from Banks Hiring Supply in Hanover Street. I still remember how my mother used to scold me for being careless. I was sometimes forced to write on the broken pieces of a slate, because of the rate at which I was breaking them.

Slates were made from fine-grain, usually bluish-grey, metamorphic rock that easily splits into thin sheets. The rectangular plates varied in size and had a wooden frame on which we could write our names. A slaty pencil was used for writing. It made a terrible, screechy noise. When writing, you had to rest one side of the slate on your chest, and support it with your other hand and arm.

Any writing on the plate was easily erased with water or a damp cloth. Miss Thutha always encouraged us to use a damp cloth rather than our wet fingers with saliva, or worse, our tongues.

One disadvantage – or advantage, depending how you looked at it – of using a slate was that you had to erase old work each time you wanted to do new work. This made it difficult for our parents to check on our progress. It also made it impossible to keep any record of your first writing exercises.

We never had organised sport at the school and we used to envy the Coloured children in the neighbourhood because they played sport at their schools and held interschool sport competitions. The only games we could play at the school were *blikkies, ikula*, hopscotch and Dutch ball.

For *blikkies* we divided into two teams. A ball and three tins were used. The three tins would be put one on top of the other and one player at a time had to throw a ball and knock down the whole lot from a certain distance. His team mates had to try to hit the other team's members with the ball before they could replace the tins.

In Dutch ball one player stood in the middle of a wide circle and the two other players tried to hit her with a ball.

One aspect of school life which we did share with the Coloured children was the feeding scheme. This we enjoyed very much. Poor as our school was, the feeding scheme was of a high standard. Fresh milk, bread, peanuts, raisins and fruit were handed out. The older pupils served us younger ones, and towards the end of the day more food was distributed for us to take home and share with our younger brothers and sisters.

Every morning we had to bring a mug to school for our milk. The milk was delivered by milk van in huge silver cans every morning after assembly. The milkman put the cans at the entrance of the school, from where four big boys carried them to the kitchen at the back.

Bread was delivered later in the day in big baskets, but the delivery men went round the back themselves to take the bread to the kitchen. The other stuff was delivered in weekly supplies and locked inside the kitchen. Only the teachers knew where to find the key!

Mr Kakaza announced when it was lunchtime. The Sub As and Bs were served first, while Miss Thutha supervised. We stood in two rows, the younger ones in front. Every pupil held their mug in their hand. First we were given bread, and then we queued for our milk. We received the food inside the classroom so the teachers could make sure that everybody had their lunch.

Towards the end of the day, during another short break, we were given peanuts, raisins or fruit, which we were taught to accept with both hands, saying, "*Enkosi.*"

School was quite a social place, because here we had the opportunity of meeting other Black children. The Black families lived spread out amongst the Coloured and other families in District Six, and as most grown-ups worked outside District Six, our parents mostly met one another through the friends we made at school. Our school mates came from all over the place, from McKenzie, Constitution, Primrose, De Villiers, William, Caledon and Stone Streets. Some other children came from further afield – from BoKaap and Woodstock, because there was only one school for Black children in central Cape Town, and it only went up to Std 2.

Black children were not allowed into Coloured schools those days, because during the early 1950s, separate education was provided for "Natives" and Coloureds – and unless someone "changed" their identity they stayed with their group. Because most of our parents did not want us to lose our identity, we were all sent to the Methodist school in Chapel Street.

It would not be long before we would visit the friends we made at school during weekends, meeting their families and starting to invite one another to birthday parties.

My brother Layton, being the only son in the family, was the only one of us who ever had a birthday party. He was six years old and about to start school. Many children were invited. One of the neighbours was kind enough to offer us his gramophone.

A big table with cakes, sweets, peanuts and potato chips was arranged at the kitchen downstairs where the party was held on the 9th of April. Decorations were made with Christmas paper and balloons. The birthday boy was sitting at the far side of the table, his face full of smiles even though there were no cards or presents. Instead, the children had brought letters with small messages and cash, as was the custom.

At one point, time was set aside for the reading of messages and the announcement of how much cash was in each envelope. We laughed at some of the funny messages. I loved "Now that you're six, you no longer look like a baboon" best!

We sang, ate, jived (to the records played on the gramophone) and played games which my sister Nombulelo organised. "Blindfold" was a favourite. The party ended at six o'clock and each little friend had a small parcel to take home. It was real fun.

Because our parents regularly met in church, after this, we all came to know each other really well, and the Black residents of District Six became a very tight-knit community.

MORE THAN JUST A MATTER OF READING AND WRITING

Mr Kakaza and Miss Thutha did not only look after our education. Every Monday those pupils who did not feel well were accompanied by Miss Thutha to a clinic in Aspeling Street. Our teacher first completed clinic cards in class for the unwell pupils. She called us individually to her table, checked if we had any sores on our heads, arms and legs. She would also put her hand on our foreheads, the method she used to check our temperature.

"Hands up, all those who want to go to the clinic today," Miss Thutha would instruct every Monday morning. After the hands had gone up, she would move her eyes around and say, "Alright then, you'll have to come to the front one by one. Let's start here," pointing to the front desk. She would take the cards, fill in the first person's name and ask, "What's your complaint today?"

"I have a stomach ache, miss," the pupil would say.

"Where is it sore? Show me." She would help by loosening the pupil's clothes. "Is it here?"

"No, miss," the child would reply.

"Where then?"

"Here, miss." Then Miss Thutha would put her hand on the little one's stomach.

"Yes, I think you must get to the clinic. Go back to your place, I'll tell you when it's time to go."

"Next!"

The next pupil would go up to the table.

Sometimes pupils told on each another.

"Miss, Sipho has a sore on his knee but he doesn't want to go to the clinic."

"Sipho!" Miss Thutha would call and check him up as well.

All the children Miss Thutha thought had a temperature had to go to the clinic. Even if we tried to convince her that there was nothing wrong with us, she would insist we go. She must have suspected that we feared the doctor's injections and would tell her that we were okay even if we weren't. A real mother she was! May her soul rest in peace.

A NEW TEACHER

When I was in Std 1, a third teacher started teaching at our school. Most of the pupils already knew Miss Mavumbe because she sang in the church choir and lived in Longmarket Street, not far from our school.

She was put in charge of Sub B and space was made available for her and her class at a hall in Clyde Street.

Sub A had grown so much that it had become impossible for Miss Thutha to handle the group any more. It was therefore decided at a parents' meeting that the school should apply for an additional teacher. This was done and the application was successful, and so Miss Mavumbe was appointed.

We knew nothing about all this and were all astonished when we saw her during assembly on the day she reported for duty. Mr Kakaza introduced her and told us the reason why she was there. All the Sub Bs were happy and delighted that they, too, were going to have a teacher of their own.

"Do you know where Clyde Street hall is?" the principal asked.

"Yes, sir," we collectively replied.

"Well, that's where Miss Mavumbe's class is going to be, because there isn't enough space here for all of us. This means that the Sub Bs will come here first on Mondays for assembly and then go to Clyde Street afterwards. But on the other days, they will go straight to Clyde Street and only come back here on Fridays at twelve o'clock. Is that clear?"

"Yes, sir," we said in unison.

Miss Mavumbe was much younger than Miss Thutha, and very active. She had a lovely figure and liked to wear tight skirts and beautiful blouses, which looked good on her. She was friendly and kind and always visited the homes of pupils who had problems.

A FUND-RAISING CONCERT

Miss Mavumbe loved choral music and she taught us a lot of songs. When funds had to be raised to pay for the hall in Clyde Street, she suggested that our school stage a concert to meet parents halfway in paying the hall fee, which was a little more than they could afford.

"Schools from outside District Six must also be invited to give musical items at the concert," she said. "The more the merrier."

Miss Mavumbe was loved by both pupils and parents because she brought many new ideas to the school.

The concert was planned for late one Friday afternoon. Tickets were printed and each pupil was given two tickets to sell, at one shilling each. Mr Kakaza told us that a prize was set aside for the pupil who sold the most tickets. So after selling the first two, pupils could ask for more.

Every day there was practice and some of the pupils had to stay behind after school, myself included, to practise. Various items were prepared for the concert – drama, choral music, drill, reciting, quartets singing Negro spirituals, and groups performing traditional dance.

On the day of the concert, all choir members were told to put on black skirts and white shirts, or white shirts, black ties and grey trousers if they were boys. It was arranged that we would arrive early and be seated before the parents and guests arrived.

That afternoon the church hall where we were taught looked transformed. The partition had been moved and placed against the back wall and the other walls had been decorated. The place looked much bigger. A stage had been built in the front and all the chairs were facing it. On the left side of the stage was a table for the chairman of the school committee and the principal to use.

At about half past four, we suddenly heard music outside the hall. We all craned our necks. Miss Mavumbe quickly slipped out of the hall. Seconds later, she came back to tell us to come and meet the guests.

Outside, the choir was singing *"Sifikile wu-u-u sifikile"* – We have arrived, wu-u-u, we have arrived. As we left the hall, we joined in the song. We stood and watched the guests, clapping our hands and singing along. The parents who were arriving stopped to watch as well.

"I-i-i-i-i," shrieked Miss Mavumbe, holding a jersey in her hand, indicating to those in the way to make space for the choir to enter the hall. The choristers were older than we were because their school went up to Std 4. They had come from Windermere by lorry and were accompanied by two teachers – the conductor, Mr Nguza, and another teacher.

As the choir was about to enter the hall, they changed song and started to sing *"Vula amasango, tsherimani, singene!"* – Open the door, chairman, and let us in! Our chairman and Mr Kakaza met them at the door where our principal greeted the two teachers and introduced them to the chairman, who acted as master of ceremonies.

The choir members, still singing, were forming a row now, moving in one step, waiting for the chairman to let them in. They were singing beautifully, especially the part where the boys begged, *"Vula, tsherimani, vula!"* – Open, chairman, open!

Then everybody went inside and was offered seats. The chairman opened the concert with a prayer, welcomed our guests and parents, and called the Chapel Street choir to the stage to render their first item. Miss Mavumbe, in a straight black skirt and a dotted black-and-white blouse, which matched our uniforms, led us onto the stage.

Our parents stood up and clapped their hands, some calling out, "Come on, Chapel Street, show them!"

This made us swell with pride and from out hearts we sang the greeting song *"Molweni, molweni iyho-yho-yho."* – Good day, good day.

"I-i-i-i-i!" went some mamas. Others shrieked, *"Halala! halala! hamba Chapel Street hamba!"* – Go, Chapel Street, go!

That really sent us going.

Mr Nguza stood next to the wall, smiling, looking satisfied at what was happening. When his choir took the stage with the song, "We don't care about other schools, Windermere is number one", everybody agreed that they were the show-stoppers.

The concert was a roaring success.

GOING TO SCHOOL IN LANGA

I did well at school, and after passing Std 2, I had to attend a township school, like all the other African children living in District Six. Along with most of the pupils who went to the Methodist school in Chapel Street, I went to Langa. I was registered at Langa Methodist school for Std 3.

I was excited that I was now also going to travel to school by train. I had always envied my two sisters who were already attending township schools.

One of the teachers at the Methodist school in Langa, Mr Lengisi, who taught Nompumelelo in Std 5, was my father's friend. I also knew him because he sometimes visited my dad during weekends. He was the one who made my parents and us children understand the importance of keeping children at school, irrespective of their gender.

It was very common in those days to take girls out of school and marry them off at an age as early as sixteen. Parents, it appeared, were enticed by the lobola, and some of them never cared to have their daughters educated beyond Std 6, so quite a number of girls left school at that stage.

Another unfortunate reason was of course the fact that most of the Black parents could not afford to pay for secondary education as they were paid very low wages and were, through the education policy of the time, forced to pay for their children's books and transport to and from school.

The first day at my new school was quite an experience. I was exposed to an altogether new environment. I felt tense, at first wondering if I would ever get used to it, in fact, wondering if a child of my age could survive it!

My new school was a five-minute walk from Langa station. The township was very different from District Six. The road from the station to the school was lined with trees. It was so peaceful and the air so fresh that I repeatedly took deep breaths.

"Is something wrong, Nomvuyo?" my sister Nompumelelo asked.

"Oh no, I'm just trying to breathe the fresh air."

"I felt the same way when I started school here. You don't get the same feeling in District Six because of the high buildings. There's a lot of open space here," Nompumelelo tried to explain.

As we approached the school, the school bell started to ring. It was a big bell hanging on a wooden frame at the end of the building. Three boys were ringing it by pulling on a long chain that was tied to it. It reminded me of the Moravian church bell back in town.

"Nompumelelo, is that the school bell?" I asked.

"Yes!" she replied. "It's big, neh?"

"Yes, and it sounds like a church bell. To think that other schools have bells this big and we didn't even have a bell in Chapel Street! I can't believe it. Look at the size of the building! I wonder which one is going to be my class," I chattered.

"The Std 3s usually use the last three classrooms, at the end," Nompumelelo said, pointing at them.

The building had two blocks of classrooms. The third wing housed the staffroom, the storeroom and the principal's office. The pupils lined up for assembly in a big open space between the two blocks. There were about six times as many pupils here as there were in the Chapel Street school.

The new school started from Sub A and continued to Std 6. There were sixteen teachers altogether, and this morning they were all standing on the stoep facing the pupils. One of the teachers conducted prayers. Then the principal came forward to make a few announcements.

He first welcomed all the new pupils, and then introduced all teachers and the standards they were going to teach that year. He also instructed all new pupils to come to his office for registration, but he promised to start with those pupils who were accompanied by their parents.

"Will there be space left for me, Nompumelelo, if I'm going to be registered last?" I asked, feeling very worried. "There are so many of us who've come to register."

"Don't worry," Nompumelelo told me. "Tata has already made arrangements with Mr Lengisi."

"How was school today, Nomvuyo?" my father asked that evening.

"I hope I won't get lost in that crowd, Tata. I've never seen such a big school, but I think I'm going to like it," I said with a smile.

Every morning I left home early for school. I had to walk down Hanover Street, then past Castle Bridge to get to the station.

At this hour, quite a number of people would be seen rushing down Hanover Street, heading for the city. Some stood at the bus stops, especially on rainy days, waiting for the Hanover Street electric tram with its overhead cables to come down the street and take them to town. Sometimes the tram's electric poles were "derailed" from the cables above, which caused a delay because the tram conductor had to take a long stick from the back and put the poles back on the cables. Whenever this happened, some of the passengers would lose patience and get off the tram and start walking.

People from District Six knew one another. They would walk in groups of threes and fours, with carry-food packets clutched to their sides, their hands in their pockets, especially on cold mornings. The young men liked to whistle as they strode down the street or waved to their friends on the opposite pavement. The clothes they wore depended on the type of job they did. Those who worked in offices dressed formally and the others, casually. Some of the older men wore blue overalls to work.

Most of the cafés were open this time of the morning for people to buy cigarettes and the morning paper. The school children on the streets at this early hour were mainly African children in their school uniforms, on their way to schools in the township – girls in black gym dresses and blouses, blue for Methodist or yellow for Anglican schools. The boys all wore white shirts and grey trousers. The school girls usually walked together, chatting about homework and other things. From whichever direction they came, most of the children met at the Grand Parade at about seven-thirty, in time for their train.

We all boarded the seven forty-five train to Langa – the same train that carried the commuters who worked the night shift at the dockyard back to the township.

At the station we had to go past a stationary train to get to the Cape Flats line – Langa station was the last stop on this line.

Out of habit we always glanced up at the timetable high up on its stand which looked a bit like a balcony and was constructed in the middle of the station on the platform that ran between the Cape Flats line and the suburban line.

On one side of the stand was a stepladder which the officer used to climb to the top to post the timetable on the big rectangular blackboard. The names of the various stations were permanently painted in white on the board, while the platform numbers were printed on smaller boards. These the officer would hang on pegs next to the name of the station, with next to it the time of departure, also written on a similar, smaller board. These small boards were put up or taken down as the officer worked on the timetable.

Delays were announced over a loudspeaker.

The commuters were always in a hurry to get back to their bachelors' quarters in Langa. They would come running onto the platform in their blue overalls, bread tins clutched under their arms, pushing aside whoever was in their way. They would glance up at the timetable for the platform number. As most of them could not read or write, you would hear them asking *"Iphi inqawa?"*– Where is the pipe?

We used to wonder what they meant by this. It was not until much later that we learnt from a friendly old man that the "pipe" described the shape of the L in the word "Langa".

How clever!

2

LIFE AT NO. 22 CROSS STREET

My father's friends from Langa used to visit us during the weekends. They tried to talk my old man into applying for a house in Langa. But he could not be convinced. He always replied that he did not want his children to grow up in a township.

"Jimmy, why don't you move from this place and try and get yourself a bigger house at Langa? Your children are getting big, you don't have enough space for your family here," I overheard one of his friends suggesting to him one day.

"Oh no!" replied my father. "I can't move from here. This place is much closer to my workplace than Langa. And another thing: I can't let my children grow up in a township."

"But, Jimmy …" another friend ventured.

"Please!" said my father. "Can we talk about something else?"

I knew he was a stubborn person and it was not going to be easy to convince him.

I was very happy that my father never gave in to his friends. I had so much fun with my friends in Cross Street. We were a small group but we knew how to enjoy ourselves.

Along the sides of our double-storeyed building ran two lanes, Dove Lane next to No. 28, and a smaller lane without a name next to No. 22.

Along the whole length of the building ran a big stoep, and all the front doors, from No. 22 to No. 28, opened on to this stoep. The windows of the first room along the passage, which ran from the front of the house to the back, also faced on to the stoep.

We liked to play hopscotch on the stoep. The only snag was that we were not allowed to play when somebody was asleep in one of the rooms, no matter how much we wanted to. But mostly we deserved to be chased away because we would make a lot of noise, arguing as soon as we felt someone was not keeping to the rules of the game.

"Out, Lillian, out!" we would yell.

"Why, what have I done?"

Often country children came to visit their city relatives – in this case the Makhabanes of Cross Street – during the festive season. They would return home before the schools reopened for the new year.

"You've stepped on the line. Look, it's still showing!"

"No ways, that line has been like that all the time."

"Alright then, lift up your foot."

Lillian did as she was instructed.

"See!"

The line of chalk clearly showed on her foot. Of course she was out.

Apart from us, there was another group who liked to use the stoep, and for something rather more serious than a hopscotch game! A group of young men from Richmond and Stuckeris Street would come, especially on Fridays, to gamble with dice, or sometimes cards. Their arguments usually ended in a fight, and on one or two occasions people actually died from stab wounds.

I still remember one Friday evening. I was just on my way out to run an errand for my mother when the sight of two men dashing at each other with knives in their hands made me stop at the front door. Their group of friends had dispersed and were watching from a distance.

"Gee my my geld! Gee my my geld!" – Give me my money! – one was shouting.

30

"Ek het dit gewen, dis nie meer joune nie," – I've won it, it's no longer yours – the other replied.

At this, the first man went beserk. He lashed out with his knife, tearing his opponent's shirt. The man staggered backwards a few steps, looked down at his shirt, then rushed forward. But he tripped over a stone and fell flat on his face. The man with the knife did not waste time. He moved in quickly and start stabbing his opponent.

"Nee man, dis nie nodig nie!" – No man, it's not necessary! – called someone, gingerly moving towards the two. But the man kept on stabbing.

There were a lot of screams and chaos, the women calling their children and trying to get them away from the scene. "Nomvuyo, come back inside and shut the door!" I heard my own mother calling. I ran inside, very frightened, and shut the front door.

I dashed upstairs to watch from the window. The man who had done the stabbing was nowhere to be seen. All I saw was the group, now surrounding the victim who was still lying on the ground. One guy knelt down, tried to turn him over and then screamed, *"Vra die babie om die ambulans te bel!"* Tell the Muslim shopkeeper to phone for an ambulance!

By the time the ambulance arrived, the man was dead and the body was covered with a white sheet.

As gambling was strictly against the law, police vans would regularly stop near our building with the intention of arresting the young offenders. But these guys were like springbok. They would disperse at the sight of the van. Often leaving all the cash behind, they would disappear down the lanes or leap over some wall to safety.

We children were aware of this and were always on the alert. We often helped ourselves to the abandoned money, usually a heap of silver coins and even a couple of bank notes.

The adults in our building did not like these men hanging about our stoep because the *tsotsis* would sometimes knock young children out of their way when fleeing from the police, hurting them badly. In the end the decision was taken that the stoep should be washed down every Friday afternoon after four o'clock, so it would be too wet to sit on.

We children took turns to scrub it with soap and water, and to our parents' delight the *tsotsis* resorted to gambling on the pavement at the corner of Cross and Richmond Streets each time they found the stoep wet.

Because we were not a big group of friends, there were both boys and girls, and we were not fussy about the games we played. The girls would play boys' games and the boys girls' games.

We always met in the evenings after supper. The first one of us to be free would stand in the street and do the dove call, using both hands. My parents knew what this meant, and without any explanation I would fly down the stairs to meet the other guys. My best friend was Gladys, whom I used to call Glad. She called me Marge instead of Marjorie, my "English" name, because at home my parents, as well as the other Black residents, called me by my first, Xhosa name, whereas my Coloured friends used my second name.

The group without Glad meant nothing to me. We were very close.

The other members of the "gang" were my brother Layton, Julie, who was Glad's younger sister, Juby and her brother Dickie, Neville and his brother Derrick, Dennis and his sister Lillian, Raymond, Albert, Lampie, Vuyani, and Audrey and her cousin Neville. A crazy mixture of a lot of Coloured and a few African children.

During the day, the most popular games were *blikkies*, Dutch ball, cricket, *huisie* and tug-of-war. In the evenings we played hide-and-seek, boys versus girls. Our hide-out was usually the Moravian church around the corner in Ashley Street. We would jump over the surrounding wall and hide amongst the trees. The problem was that we had to hide from both the boys and the church's night watchman! The old man patrolled the garden and at the slightest noise would shine a torch around the place. The boys were clever.

While Glad whispered, "Come this way, Marge. Where are the others?" and Juby urged, "Hush, there's somebody coming, I can see his torch light! Keep still!" the boys would be laughing loudly on the other side of the wall, calling out to the watchman, "Watchie! Watchie, there are thieves in the churchyard!" At which point, we were forced to give ourselves up.

Afterwards we would sit down in a corner of the stoep and tell stories.

We discovered quite a lot of things during story-time. In the lane next to No. 22 we sometimes picked up what we thought were balloons. To our surprise we noticed that any adult who saw us play with these "balloons" would scream, "Throw that filthy stuff away! Immediately."

We always wondered why our parents reacted this way because none of them ever explained to us what the balloons were. Only much later did the older brother of one of the group members tell him what the actual use of the "balloons" was. We still didn't quite understand.

During story-time we talked about our school work and our families. We shared problems and even discussed the teenagers in the area who had started dating. This is where I discovered how different the Coloured schools were from ours. I learnt about their facilities, the types of sport they played, the names of their teachers and how they treated them. Most of our gang – Glad, Julie, Neville, Raymond, Juby and Audrey – attended school at George Golding in Walmer Estate.

Even the boys talked about ballet, something which was not part of our school experience and we hardly knew about. We, on the other hand, told them about our music evenings and the different games we played at school. They did not know any African games, like *imbongolo*, for instance.

Imbongolo was played by girls only. Actually, the "imbongolo" means mule. A group of girls would sit in a circle holding a stone about the size of a small fist, in their hands. They would rhythmically thump the stone on the ground, singing:

Mbongolo we mbongolo
Mbongolo we mbongolo

Then the song changed to:

Ibigqith'aph'imbongolo
Ibigqith'aph'imbongolo
It passed here, the mule
It passed here, the mule

In time to the singing, the stones were passed to the next player in the circle, and if anybody missed the beat, she had to stop playing.

This kind of game was very different from those our gang in Cross Street shared.

TALKING OF CULTURAL DIFFERENCES

Without us realising it, a lot of cultural differences came up in our story-telling sessions. Even marriage customs.

It amazed us, for instance, that in the Coloured community, the husband would stay with the in-laws, whereas exactly the opposite happens in the African community. And the different wedding ceremonies! I had never heard of going on honeymoon, and Glad didn't know about *ukuhota*, the period immediately after the wedding when the bride has to pay respect to the elders of the husband's family; when she is taught *hlonipha* – the terms of respect she is to use towards the male members of the husband's family.

During this time, Glad was surprised to hear, the bride also learns which household items she may not use, like the father-in-law's plates, and which areas around the homestead she may traditionally not enter, like the kraal.

We were told about the circumcision of Muslim boys when they are very young, and we stunned our Coloured friends by telling them about the initiation school which African youths attend when they are about eighteen. They were also circumcised, but then along with a group of youths their own age, who will be sent "to the bush" and isolated in *amabhuma*, small huts, to prepare them for manhood.

Sometimes we used to ask each other really stupid questions, like, "What is one and one in your school?"

What a joke it was to discover that the answer was the same!

In winter, when it was too cold to meet on the stoep, we liked to organise a *mbawula*, a big tin, and make fire. We would put the tin on the pavement and stand around it, the boys and girls taking turns to fetch wood to feed the fire.

One cold evening, while we were sitting around the fire, Dickie came running up, holding something big covered with newspaper.

"Make way!" he shouted.

We thought he had brought a log of wood and gratefully started to move aside because the fire was starting to die down.

But instead of a log, it was a big black cat! Everybody started screaming.

Dickie nevertheless chucked the cat into the tin. Fortunately he missed. Only a part of the cat's tail caught fire. The poor animal mewed with shock and we jumped back, giving it a chance to escape.

"Dickie!" Juby shouted. "What on earth do you think you're doing!"

"It's not funny!" Neville exclaimed. "You're cruel, do you know that?"

We were not impressed. It was a stroke of luck that the poor animal did not get hurt. Cats really have nine lives.

Most Black women belonged to Christian women's groups. Mrs Nokhubeka of William Street (2nd from left in front row) was among the committee members of the Women's *Manyano* of the Bantu Presbyterian Church, as it was then called. From the inscriptions on the tablecloth it is clear that even in the early sixties, the different languages (Xhosa, English, Sotho and Afrikaans) were recognised and respected in District Six.

Glad taught me a lot of things: how to ride a bicycle and how to swim. Every morning during the school holidays she had to take her brother's lunch to his workplace in Woodstock. She used to take me along to the factory on the bicycle, and on our way back she would give me a chance to ride.

The first time I was on a bicycle I had difficulty in sitting up straight.

"Don't lie on one side, Marge, try and sit up straight," Glad advised.

She held the bicycle from behind, at the back of the seat, while I tried to steer. Heaven knows how many times I fell off. It took me more than a week to get it right.

"Guess what?" I said to my brother.

Layton looked at me as if trying to read my mind. "Whatever it is, it must be good," he said.

"I can ride a bicycle," I announced. "Glad taught me. Today I rode all the way from Woodstock up to Stuckeris Street. She was running behind me all the way."

"I don't believe you!"

"Ask her. I have been practising for the past two weeks."

"Tata will kill you if he discovers that you're riding other children's bicycles," Layton warned.

"Kill me? Come on! You're just jealous. I know that Tata won't mind," I said. "I can ride a bicycle and you can't, that's all," I added.

And it turned out I was right. Layton was indeed worried that he could be outclassed by a girl. Raymond, his friend, came to his rescue and let him practise on his bike in the parking area in front of the Trafalgar swimming pool. In less than two weeks, he was just as good as I was.

I found swimming fascinating, though it was uncommon for young Black girls to swim in public.

Glad gave me swimming lessons at the Trafalgar swimming pool. We visited the pool regularly during the school holidays. It was three feet deep at one end and seven feet (just over two meters) at the other. At the deep end, there were two diving boards, a high and a low one. Expert swimmers used this side, and it was fun to lie in the sun and watch them diving. Some of them loved to show off.

One day a young weight-lifter named Niel was walking round the edges of the pool, posing so that the onlookers could admire his body. Later he strolled to the high diving board, climbed up the ladder and on top pretended to test the board by jumping lightly up and down. At last he took a beautiful dive into the sparkling blue water. But instead of Niel coming up, the water turned red.

The onlookers started screaming. The life-savers immediately dived into the pinky-red water and brought him up. The limp body was taken out of the water. First aid was applied, but there was no response. After a while Niel's body was covered with bath towels and an ambulance took him to hospital, where he was certified dead on arrival: he had hit his head on the bottom of the pool and broken his neck. Poor fellow!

After that we stayed away from the pool for a few months. Glad could not get over the shock because she knew Niel well. They were classmates at one stage, she told me, and used to sit next to each other in class.

"He was always so protective when the other boys teased me," she said. "I can't believe that he died just like that, right in front of everybody."

My brother was not so worried about Niel's death as such, he was more worried that my father would never allow us to go near the pool again if he heard about the accident, so we never said anything of the sad incident to my parents!

CHURCH AND BIBLE STUDY

On Sunday mornings the church service was conducted at the Mission. Miss Matthews, a Coloured lady from Horstley Street, was the Sunday school teacher. She was a devoted Christian, never absent and never late. She would come down Dove Lane with her guitar under her arm and unlock the church hall. When she started singing, the old people in the neighbourhood would slowly gravitate towards the hall.

The proper service started at ten o'clock, but at half past nine we children would already go inside to listen to Miss Matthews telling Bible stories with the help of a green flannel board on which she stuck cut-out figures. These cut-out figures had pieces of flannel at the back which enabled them to stick to the board. As she related the Bible stories, the different characters got stuck on the board. At the end of the story all the characters would be there – Jesus and all twelve apostles, if it was a story from the New Testament; perhaps Moses and the snake of gold high up on a pole in front of the Children of Israel, if the story came from the Old Testament.

The group in the church were of various ages; the majority of children were Coloured, with very few Africans. Though the community was generally poor, we dressed up for Sunday school and knew exactly how to conduct ourselves during class and inside the Mission. At the end of each lesson, Miss Matthews asked questions, or sometimes she would ask one of the bigger children to come in front and retell the story.

Then she would play the guitar. She sang beautifully. My favourite chorus was:

Jesus died for all the children
All the children of the world
Red and yellow black and white
All are precious in his sight
Jesus died for all the children of the world

At three o'clock in the afternoon it would be the turn of three White people, Mr Alexander and two ladies, to come to the church hall to teach us about the Bible. They always came by car, with the boot loaded full of loaves of bread. During the service we were divided into three groups according to age.

Mr Alexander was in charge of the older group. His class was more organised than Miss Matthews's because apart from story-telling, we also read from the Bible. Every Sunday he handed out small cut-out pictures with quotations from the Bible which we pasted into medium-sized, blank books with our names on. These books were kept by Mr Alexander and handed out each time we had to paste in some more pictures. One could tell the number of times each child attended Sunday school by the number of pictures in the book. At the end of the year, the best attender was given a prize.

After the afternoon service, everybody would be given a loaf of bread to take home.

"Another loaf of bread from Mr Alexander?" my mother would ask as we walked in with the bread tucked under one arm. "Put it away for tomorrow's sandwiches, it is most appreciated."

Mr Alexander and the two ladies always returned on Tuesday evenings to hold Bible study at Mrs Ntshiba's place, upstairs at No. 26.

The Bible study was attended mostly by older people, but a few children also attended, myself included. We usually sat around the table so that we could be near the paraffin lamp that stood in the middle of the table, because we read a lot from the Bible. Older people were given a chance to pray and the children said the Lord's Prayer.

Mr Alexander encouraged us children to read verses from the Bible. We took turns in doing this, and later on he would ask us to answer questions from the read passage.

One evening Mr Alexander wanted to know from us what we understood by "eternal life". Audrey stood up and boldly said, "If Table Mountain was made of rice and one grain was taken away each time a year went by, that would almost be like eternal life because it would take many, many years to remove all the grains."

"Good," Mr Alexander said, smiling.

What was interesting was the fact that nobody ever gave a wrong answer, as long as they could explain why they thought their answer was right.

I think Mr Alexander's approach developed our minds a lot. Much later, I used to get good marks in critical analysis at teachers' training college!

END-OF-YEAR SUNDAY PICNIC

At the end of each year we were given a treat by Mr Alexander and the two ladies. They would hire a bus to take us to a picnic spot of their choice.

The day of the picnic used to be great fun. Mr Alexander would tell us the itinerary for the day. This meant that everybody knew exactly what to do, and when. We would all dress informal on this day. Before we went off for the picnic we would be divided into groups of eight, and each group would nominate their leader, usually from the older children.

Mr Alexander would drive a bakkie instead of his usual car on the Sunday of the picnic. The bakkie would come loaded with boxes at the back, together with a basket full of bread rolls, cases of drinks and firewood. Everybody would sit on the pavement next to the Mission door waiting for Mr Alexander to come down Richmond Street. At the sight of the bakkie, the smaller children would scream, "Here comes Mr Alexander! Here comes Mr Alexander!"

Mr Alexander would joyfully hoot to announce his arrival. Not long after this, the bus would arrive.

As soon as the bus arrived, Mr Alexander and the bigger boys would load the stuff from the van on to the bus. The two ladies would in the meantime help the smaller children and girls board, and the bus driver would assist them. Of course everybody rushed to sit next to a window.

As soon as everybody had boarded, the driver would start the engine and we would all try to look out of the windows, waving good-bye to our parents, who would be standing on stoeps or sometimes at the windows, waving back to us, shouting, *"Mooi loop!"* – Go well!

The first thing we did as we arrived at the picnic spot was to stand in a circle, with Mr Alexander in the middle. He would pray, thanking the Lord for the safe journey. After that, the boys would unload all the stuff from the bus and put it down next to one of the tables. Mr Alexander would then organise the fires in the braai places while the two ladies and the bigger girls started buttering the breadrolls.

Lunchtime was usually the nicest treat. We used to sit on the lawn, friends together, and enjoy the meal, each child having received a plate with a big piece of meat, two breadrolls, salads and a bottle of cool drink. It was common to hear children remark that they had never been given such a lot of meat.

Even during leisure time we would break, sit down and talk about the Lord.

Then we split into groups and played games. Mr Alexander taught us how to play volleyball, girls versus boys. While the two ladies held the rope we would hit the ball across and try and catch our opponents unawares. We used to laugh with each other each time the opponents missed the ball. Afterwards we might play tug-of-war or hide-and-seek. If there were any see-saws, merry-go-rounds or swings around, the younger children clambered all over them. By four o'clock we would all be tired from the games and happy to go home, the winners of the games with their prizes – small dolls, toy motorcars, books with pictures, and ordinary storybooks.

Nobody felt left out, for at the end of the day, everybody would be a winner: everyone had something to take home.

HOLIDAY TIME

After the picnic Sunday there would be only one Sunday left for Mr Alexander's Sunday school before we closed for the December vacation. This meant that we now had the Sunday afternoons to ourselves. So during the end-of-year holidays we took long walks after lunch to the Gardens in the centre of Cape Town where we sat on the benches and watched the birds and squirrels. Or we strolled in the Gardens, pausing at the fish pond to watch the goldfish.

We lingered in the cool shade, listening to the birds in the trees and enjoying the peace and quiet of the open spaces, which was different from the crowded, noisy streets of District Six.

Sometimes we would go into the museum to look at the Bushmen and amuse ourselves with the big, stuffed gorilla.

"Dennis, what would you do if you woke up one morning and found yourself turned into a gorilla?" Neville jokingly asked on one such visit.

Dennis stared at the gorilla and said, *"Die lelike ding!* – The ugly thing. I would ask my parents to take me to the zoo and throw me into the lion's den."

"Ha! ha! ha!" everybody laughed.

"I don't think the lions would even dream of eating you if you're this ugly," Layton said, pulling a face at the gorilla. "Unless of course, they didn't have anything to eat that day."

Albert Makhabane and a friend on their way to the (Company) Gardens in the centre of Cape Town. Watching the birds and squirrels in the Gardens – and especially the stuffed gorilla in the nearby SA Museum – was a favourite pastime with us on Sundays when there was no Sunday school.

We cracked up laughing again.

"It's easy," said Glad. "They can cover your face so that the lions won't lose their appetite. *Man, die ding is lelik!*" – Man, the thing *is* ugly!

We all laughed so loud that the man in charge walked over to us and very sternly said, "I will have to ask you to leave."

We decided to get out before we were thrown out.

The next Sunday we went to the Rhodes Memorial above the University of Cape Town instead and fed bananas to the baboons in the cages.

3

ENTERTAINMENT OUR STYLE

"Marge, which film are you going to see tomorrow?" asked Glad one Friday afternoon.

"I don't know," I said, a note of misery in my voice. "I'm not even sure I'm going to the movies tomorrow."

"Hey? Come on, why?" Glad asked, pushing me with a smile.

"I only have eight pennies. So unless somebody sends me on an errand and gives me a tip ..."

"Okay, let's not worry about that, it's still Friday. Let's see what we can do."

We were then approached by Neville, eating a big, juicy mango.

"Neville, what's showing at the Star tomorrow?" asked Glad.

"I'm not sure. I think I'm going to the British – *To Hell and Back!*"

"What's that all about?" I asked.

"War."

"Sorry, not for me. I don't like war films!" I replied.

"Marge, let's go to the Avalon. They're showing *Tammy and the Bachelor*," suggested Glad.

"Good, the Avalon then."

"You girls, you like old-fashioned films. What do you know about love? I'm going to organise the boys that we go to the British," Neville said.

"That's fine with us," replied Glad. "Can we have a bite from your mango? You seem to be enjoying every bit of it."

"Sure, it's nice." And Neville handed Glad the remaining piece. He turned to go.

"I hope you stay in hell and don't come back!" I called after him.

Neville pretended not to hear and joined Dennis, who was just on his way back from the shop.

"Julie has seen *To Hell and Back*," Gladys whispered to me. "She says it' a movie for boys, not girls." So we agreed: we had taken the right decision. All that was left was to convince the other girls to join us.

We were very fond of going to the movies as a group, because we liked to discuss the film on the stoep later, during story-time. That was another reason why it was a good idea for the boys to go to a different movie, because it meant that we would have two different films to share. We were disappointed, though, the next day when the boys said that they could not tell the story because it was just a lot of shooting and killing.

"It was a long, boring film," said Derrick.

"Oh, shut up! What do you know about boring films? You're still young!" Neville shouted.

The argument went on. Glad stopped them just when Neville was on the point of losing his temper.

"*Tammy and the Bachelor* was quite interesting," I said, trying to change the subject. It worked because the girls immediately started to brag about their right choice.

"You boys missed a lot. You should have seen how pretty and young Debbie Reynolds looked for the bachelor," boasted Glad.

"Was Tammy Debbie Reynolds?"

"Yes, and the bachelor was ... er, who was that guy, Glad?" Audrey enquired. "Quite handsome, I must say," she added, giving Neville a sideways glance.

"Leslie Nielsen!"

"Of course!" remembered Audrey. "Anyway, we really enjoyed it."

"I still feel that girls enjoy films about love and romance more than boys. Except for my younger brother here," said Neville, putting his hand on Derrick's head. Derrick angrily shook his brother's hand off. Neville pretended not to notice. "I think we older guys enjoyed *To Hell and Back.*"

That was the last word on the topic.

Sometimes we went to see the same movies. The Star bioscope was where we mostly went, because it was cheaper and only a five-minute walk from Cross Street.

But apart from being the nearest, it was not as well organised as the Avalon, and you paid as you entered. Unlike the Avalon, no bookings were allowed. This arrangement suited us fine because it meant that some of us could get in without paying. What we did was to give our money to Glad to buy all the tickets. We would then quickly rush in, telling the usher that the tickets were with Glad and that she was behind us. By the time he discovered that he had been tricked, we were safely inside. But they never really bothered to check on us, especially our favourite usher, Sakkie, who was kind and used to dealing with children. Anyway, we were old patrons.

At the front entrance of the Avalon was an iron gate which opened directly on to the foyer. This gate was used to regulate the flow of patrons.

As soon as a reasonable number of movie-goers were inside, the gate-keeper, a tall Muslim guy with a big stomach, would shut the gate to give the people in the foyer time to buy their tickets and be ushered into the hall. Then he would let in the next lot.

Because he was so strong, the gate-keeper always managed to shut his gate, even if the patrons were pushing from outside. Our gang nicknamed him Goofy, and we would not say to each other, "Don't be late for the movies!" – we said, "Don't let Goofy shut you out!"

The Star was very big, much bigger than the Avalon. In spite of its size, we never dared to use the back seats, because this part of the cinema would be occupied by the Globe gang. The members of the gang, whose name originated from the name of a furniture shop nearby – The Globe Furnishing Company – were dagga smokers. The heavy, pungent smoke that drifted from the back row irritated us a lot. It burnt our eyes and choked us, but the ushers never did anything about it.

Opposite the Star cinema was a fish market: a row of fish stalls which sold fish fresh from the sea – hake, snoek, maasbankers and even cray-fish. On the opposite corner of the fish market was a fishery, an ordinary fish shop, where you could buy fish and chips, also cool drinks, bread and breadrolls.

Part of the fun of going to double-feature movies was to buy fish and chips and bread at the fishery during interval. But you had to stand in such long queues that sometimes, by the time you got back to the cine-ma with your steaming fish, the second film would already be showing. Because we did not all want to miss a part of the film, we took turns to buy the fish and come in late. Nobody worried about us eating the fish and chips and bread while we were watching the movie – and nobody worried about us informing the buyer of the fish what had happened in his or her absence.

On Saturday evenings we stayed up until late in order to listen to Top Twenty over the radio. Raymond had a battery-operated portable radio which he got from his mother for his birthday. He used to bring it along to the stoep. There was no way we would have been allowed to sit inside someone's home and listen to the hit parade, because none of our parents would let us do what we enjoyed most – sing along with the music, and dance.

We knew nearly every record on the hit parade, and as soon as the pre-senter mentioned the name of the record and its position, we started singing, for instance, "The Shadows Dance On", a song by Paul and Paula; Elvis Presley's "Return to Sender"; or Cliff Richard's "Bachelor Boy".

We took turns guessing the order in which the hits would come and in-sisted on singing along with our favourites, even though we often sang out of tune. Juby had a lovely voice, though, and she and Raymond used to sing Paul and Paula's duet beautifully. The rest of us would start clapping our hands and dancing to the tune, encouraging them to go on. It was real fun!

GUY FAWKES

My mother's birthday was on Guy Fawkes Day. So instead of us buying her presents, she bought us fireworks. On the evening of the 5th of November, we would all come out in the street with our fireworks, dividing into a boys' and a girls' group.

We girls put all our fireworks together and in turn each was given a "cricket". Someone would be assigned to have a match ready and set it alight. Crickets looked like birthday candles, only shorter, and they blew out as soon as they were lit. Each of us got a chance to throw a cricket at the boys, but you had to very fast if you did not want it blowing out in your hand.

Some of us would get burnt and cry, but that was all in the game. We would wipe our tears and return to watch the firing of the sky rockets, which were lit by adults. The rockets were usually put in empty bottles so that they would go up straight. It was great fun watching them shoot up and burst into different colours in the sky.

One Guy Fawkes Day, however, fate gave my mother the worst present that she could ever have asked for. Layton had already lit all his fireworks during the day. Come evening, when the gang started their usual sports, he did not have a single cricket or cracker. He stood there looking on, his eyes full of envy. We had no sympathy with him and refused to share our our fireworks with him. So he went to Mama, who asked Nompumelelo to go and buy some more crackers.

I accompanied Nompumelelo and Layton to the shop. My reason for going along was to try and trick Nompumelelo into buying more fireworks for me as well. We went to the shop at the corner of Stuckeris and Hanover Streets because they stocked a large variety of fireworks.

Nompumelelo handed the fireworks to Layton to carry. We were in a great hurry to get back home, so she rushed out of the shop and raced across Hanover Street – too fast for me to follow. I stood on the pavement to wait for a car to pass when I heard the screeching of brakes, and loud screams. I looked across and, yes, there was no mistake! It was Nompumelelo. My sister had been run over by the car!

The screams brought all the customers out of the shop.

I cried, "Nompumelelo! Nompumelelo!" and looked around to check on

Layton but I could not see him anywhere. Then I sprinted across the street, a bit confused, not knowing whether I should run home and tell my mother or stay with Nompumelelo.

I was stamping my feet and crying. I remember a Coloured lady grabbing my arm and saying, "Run home quickly and tell your mother!" She also looked very upset.

So I ran up Richmond Street and met my mother halfway with Tat'-uBenya, Ngele and Makupula. They had already heard. Layton had told them.

"Nomvuyo!" my mother called when she saw me. "Where is Nompumelelo, where is my child Nompumelelo?"

"She's been run over by a car, Mama!" I replied, crying.

We all ran back to the spot of the accident. Nompumelelo was still under the car when we got there. The driver was a very fair, middle-aged Coloured man who could easily have been mistaken for a White. He was the type that was sometimes referred to as "amper baas". At this point he was as white as a sheet, of course. With a trembling voice he begged the bystanders to help him lift the car so that they could get my sister out from underneath the right front wheel.

Two young Coloured men were kneeling down, looking under the car and trying to pull her out. Tat'uBenya, Ngele and Makupula did not hesitate. They rushed forward.

The shopkeeper, Mr Abrahams, ran back into his shop and quickly phoned for the police and ambulance.

We all thought that Nompumelelo was dead. My mother and I and some other women were standing on the pavement, watching, frantic with worry.

Then we heard Nompumelelo cry. We were so relieved. At least she was alive! Suddenly my mother started screaming. It must have been from delayed shock. A neighbour ran and fetched a glass of sugar water for her, and after a while she calmed down.

Just before they got Nompumelelo out from underneath the car, the police and the ambulance arrived. The upper part of her body was free from the car now, but every time the two young men tried to pull the rest out, she started screaming.

"Nee, nee, wag!" the police cautioned. *"Lig die kar en stoot hom terug!"* So four policemen, three of our neighbours, the driver and the two young men managed to lift the car and push it back. The ambulance men attended to Nompumelelo as soon as the car was out of the way.

After a quick examination, the driver of the ambulance approached my mother and said, "I'm sorry, mama, she can't go home with you. We have to take her to hospital. There is something wrong with her left leg. Can I have her name and address, please?"

After he had taken down the information in a pocket book, the driver said, "We're taking her to Victoria Hospital in Wynberg."

Nompumelelo was put on a stretcher and carried into the ambulance. I was crying softly, holding on to my mother's dress. I burst into tears at the sound of the siren as the ambulance went down Stuckeris Street.

The only thing that kept my family going that evening was the support we got from our neighbours.

It was the first time that I saw my father cry. He was not around when the accident happened. He had to go to his younger brother, Benjamin, after work. When he arrived home from Kensington where his brother lived, he was shocked to find the house full of neighbours.

I still remember him entering the room. Startled, he looked around. I suppose he saw my mother first because he asked, "Where are my children?"

Tat'uMakupula asked him to take a seat. Then he slowly said, "Jimmy, there's been an accident. Nompumelelo has been run over by a car, but she's alright. She's been taken to hospital."

My father paused for a minute. Then he said, "Please tell me if she's dead." The tears started to roll down his cheeks.

"No, no, she's not dead, Jimmy. She's just hurt her leg. She's been taken to Victoria Hospital."

"Can you tell me what happened?" my father said, wiping his eyes with a handkerchief.

My mother told him the story with heavy sighs in between.

My father did not say anything after this. Tat'uMakupula led us in prayer, and after that the neighbours started to leave.

It turned out that my sister had broken her left femur in several places. She had to stay in hospital for more than three months. On her first day home an evening prayer was held for her, and some of the neighbours joined our family to give thanks to the Lord.

THE FESTIVE SEASON

Christmas time was a busy time for all of us. All the neighbours in the street would be rushing around, purchasing paint from Levine in Longmarket Street and cleaning their walls. New sets of curtaining would be bought and windows washed before the curtains were hung.

Right through the year the residents of No. 22 Cross Street saved money for Christmas groceries by buying Christmas stamps. At the beginning of the year we joined a Christmas club and received a booklet for the stamps and a catalogue which offered different grocery packages.

All the items in a particular package were listed, with the total value underneath.

The stamps were purchased from those shopkeepers in Hanover Street who were agents for the Christmas clubs, and pasted in the stamp booklet, so that the pages were slowly filled up with rows of little Christmas trees or tiny Father Christmases on a sledge.

When their booklets were full, which was usually towards Christmas, our parents would take them to the clubs and in return get boxes and boxes of groceries containing corned beef, rice, samp, fish oil, sugar, flour, jelly, custard powder, raisins, sweets.

The foodstuffs were used throughout the festive season. Fancy Christmas dinners would be prepared. Housewives shared recipes and cooked special dishes. The Black housewives learnt a lot from their Coloured friends in the neighbourhood. African people regarded salad and pudding dishes in particular as "Western" food, and hardly ever served them.

Our normal diet during the year was stampmealies, beef, mutton or chicken, fresh vegetables, rice, and *umvubo* in summer. *Umvubo*, made from mealiemeal, is prepared with less water than "stywe pap". It is also call it *umphokoqo*, or "krummelpap". *Umphokoqo* or *umvubo* would be cooled first before being prepared with creamy *amasi* – sour milk – in a dish. This African dish was used a lot on sunny days because it was served cold.

Our Christmas dishes were, however, much fancier. My mother used to prepare a variety of meat dishes. We would have rolled beef, which she pot-roasted with potatoes, as well as roast chicken. There would also be rice, fresh vegetables and beetroot salad. We had jelly and custard, as well, and "mixed" drinks, like Oros and water.

Christmas day was really a day for the family, and we had to stick to our family's programme, so the members of the gang did not see each other. Instead, we would be invited out with our families.

Glad's family would be away most of the day, visiting her eldest brother in Walmer Estate. I would have lunch with my family and then afterwards join my Black friends Puleni, Siziwe, Princess and Esther. Together we would visit all the Black families we knew around District Six, wishing them a good Christmas. We drifted from the Mgudlwas in Caledon Street to the Mahlangenis in Ashley Street; from the Fuzanis in Roger Street to the Madlingozis in Combrinck Street and the Mgunculus in Hanover Street.

Everybody was in a good mood and we were given all kinds of sweets – toffees, "icy mints", lollipops, chocolates – and sometimes even a penny or two.

The first thing we would do was knock at the door.

Knock! Knock!

"Come in," a voice inside would call.

"We're bringing Christmas greetings."

"Oh! Come in, come in, how many are you?"

What was interesting about the adults we visited was that they made sure that each child received the same amount of money.

"Happy Christmas, children. Thank you for coming by. We're going to give you one shilling. How many did you say you were?"

If the number was odd, they would get more money and make it even.

"Alright, this is one shilling and you are six, so each one will get two-pence. Here you are!" And each one of us would be given their share, and we would all accept it with both hands, saying, "*Enkosi*, mama," or, "*Enkosi*, tata."

The adults liked to remark about the way we looked, but they would never compare us. "You all look beautiful today, who bought you these beautiful clothes?" they would say.

"Our parents!" we would collectively reply. "Thank you for the Christmas gift."

Then we would leave.

Others would ask us to sing before they gave us something. This of course was no problem. Esther led us in her beautiful voice and we sang the "action songs" we learnt at school, making gestures with our hands and talking with our eyes.

Our parents always bought us new clothes at this time of the year. Everybody would be in new attire on Christmas day and the church in Chapel Street would be bursting at its seams with children showing off their new clothes. After the sermon we would rush out, talk to one another and admire the outfits.

"Where was your dress bought?" you would sometimes dare to ask.

And the name of the shop would be shyly given.

Some of the little girls wore bows in their hair, but most of the children kept their hair short.

BOXING DAY AT THE BEACH

On Boxing Day, the day after Christmas, just about every Black youth in District Six went to Muizenberg beach. My parents never took us to the beach but on Boxing Day they allowed us to go.

"Tata, why don't you and Mama ever join us at the beach?" Layton once asked.

"No, my child, we can't go to the seashore."

"Why not?" I wanted to know.

"Come on, children, run along now and stop asking questions," my mother intervened.

"But, Mama," I protested.

"Alright, alright, I'll tell you when you come back," my father promised.

That evening just after supper my brother started again. "Tata, haven't you forgotten something?"

"Yes, Tata, you promised," I reminded him.

"The story of the sea being sacred and healing is an old one," my father finally began. "If you learnt your history, you will remember that when the White people arrived at the Cape during the seventeenth century they only came into contact with the African people in the interior, not near the coast. This shows that the African people always had an interest in agriculture, but also, that they always respected the sea and would never live next to the coast. Do you know that twins also, are forbidden to go to the sea?"

"Twins! Why is that so, Tata?" Layton asked, looking very surprised.

"These things are not questioned, especially by children. Listen to what your father's telling you and stop asking questions," my mother interrupted. "Do you know what?" she continued. "When I was your age my parents told me that girls should not eat eggs. I wasn't allowed to ask the reason why; all I did was to stay away from eggs. That is how we were brought up! And that is how I'm going to bring you up!"

"I think your mother is right," my father said quietly.

I looked at my brother. I could see he was disappointed, but he did not say anything. Sensing trouble, I also kept quiet.

"Another thing. It's time for prayer now," my mother continued, deliberately putting an end to the conversation.

Though our parents never went to Muizenberg, they asked the young people who did go to take along empty bottles and fill them with sea water. So when we returned in the late afternoon, just about everyone had a bottle of sea water with them. This, we discovered, the adults used as an enema.

What we could not understand was why the sea water could not be taken inside the house.

"It will lose its magic power of healing," we were always told. So the bottles of sea water never entered the house but were taken through the back gate and placed in the backyard to be used in the outside toilet.

Hardly anybody in District Six had an inside toilet, and even if we'd had one, the emptying of the stomach would have to be done away from the house, maybe in the veld somewhere.

We went to Muizenberg by train. We had to get up at the crack of dawn to catch an early train because after eleven o'clock the trains would be chock-a-block – even though the railway transport service adjusted the normal timetable during this time of the year to make sure that more trains ran on the line between Cape Town and Simonstown.

Still, people experienced a lot of discomfort on the trains, and sometimes fights broke out among the passengers. Christmas was a time of love and peace, but if the trains were so overcrowded there was suddenly a lack of tolerance. So the earlier you got to Muizenberg and back the safer.

The first time I went to Muizenberg beach I was with my two sisters. We got up early and took along some food which my mother had prepared. When the train stopped at Mowbray station I could not believe that all the people waiting on the platform wanted to board the train too! There was chaos and a lot of noise. Most of the people were from Langa. Small wonder my mother was not so keen to let my sisters take me along! A child of my age could easily get lost in that crowd.

We got off at Muizenberg station and walked for a long distance because the area next to the station was reserved for Whites only. At last we reached the area for Black people and found a good spot under a bridge. I took off my clothes, put on my bathing suit and ran into the sea with the beach ball that my mother had brought me from her work. I made a lot of friends within a short time and we enjoyed ourselves in the water, throwing and catching the ball.

NEW YEAR

New Year was the best. It was Coon Carnival in District Six and young and old loved to watch. Even the township residents flocked to town, and we always had visitors from Langa who did not want to miss this unique type of entertainment.

We carried benches and chairs to Hanover Street to sit on and watched from afternoon till evening. Quite a number of adults from Cross Street came down to watch with us children.

Sometimes we would get to Tat'uCakwe's place, a family friend who stayed in Stuckeris Street and had one door of his room leading onto a balcony. This was the most convenient place to watch the troupes. From here we could communicate with the other children down in the street and tell them which troupes were coming.

The music, sometimes taken from the records on the hit parade, was very fast – in time with the trotting of the troupes. Some of the songs were unique to the this time of year, like "Daar kom die Alabama", "January, February, March, …" and "Ek dans met die meisie met die kortste rokkie".

The various groups would come down Hanover Street, trotting and prancing and dancing in their bright, shiny satin costumes. We knew the colours and could recognise the Coon troupes from afar: the Pennsylvanians, the Dahomeys, the Bits and Pieces, the Philadephians, the Haarlem Darkies, Spes Bona.

The troupes would march all the way down to the centre of Cape Town, right up Wale Street to the BoKaap and on, to Green Point, where they held their singing and marching competitions.

The highlight of the day was when they returned, still marching and performing like mad. We would count the glittering trophies each group had won as they pranced past.

Our favourite troupe were the Dahomeys in their mustard-and-brown uniforms. The leader used do dress up as a woman and swung his hips just like a flirt when he marched. The troupe had so many members and made such loud music that you could hear them approach from afar. Quite a lot of school-going boys whom we knew joined them because they had such a good following in the community.

The Dahomeys always fared well in the competitions and would bring back a number of trophies.

The Atchers were also an entertaining group, but young children were scared stiff of this group of "devils", all dressed up in red with small devils' horns on their heads and a forked tail swinging from the back of their pants. The little ones would start clinging to their mothers as soon as they heard the distant drum. But sometimes the adults would hear the drum first and call out, *"Hier kom die Atchers!"* – Here come the Atchers!, whereupon the children would frantically try to hide from sight.

It was easy to recognise the Atchers because they did not sing like the other troupes. All they did was beat the drum, jump about and yell like Red Indians, doing their best to scare the onlookers. So even older children would quietly move around, sneaking away from the *voorloper* who leapt about in front of the marching band, his red satin outfit glinting in the light and the long fork in his hand sending a chill down the bravest child's spine.

NO MORE DOVE CALLS IN THE EVENING

When we were in our mid-teens a terrible thing happened. Glad's mother fell ill and became bed-ridden. This was a blow, not only to her family, but to our entire group. Glad used to be the life and soul of the gang, so when she could no longer spend time with us because she had to look after her mother, we started to drift apart. It was a terrible shock for me when Glad told me one day, "We're going to move to a bigger house in Kensington."

After Glad's family moved away, the gang members stopped seeing each other regularly and started to have different interests. Juby started to date. She dropped out of school and got work in a factory and never bothered herself with school-going kids again.

The boys began to stick together, playing boys' games, so that we girls were totally out of the picture.

My brother and I started to spend a lot of time on our school work. We joined study groups, and because the different race groups had to attend different schools, only African pupils could be members of our study group. I became closer to my Langa school mates and saw less and less of my old Coloured friends.

The dove call in the evenings was no more.

This picture of me and some friends was taken at Thomas Street. On the left is Nomalady, daughter of the famous rugby player Ivan Fuzani; Siziwe can just be seen to the left of me, while Nomathemba (whose photograph this is) gives a typical broad smile; to her right is Sophia, who later left for Johannesburg, and finally Notuna, who still lives in Guguletu where her parents, like those of the other girls, were moved to in 1963.

4

GOING TO THE COUNTRY FOR CHRISTMAS

When I was young, it was common practice for Black people in and around big cities to spend the festive season with their families in the country. We called this *ukugoduka*.

The same was true for the residents of No. 22 Cross Street.

It was customary for any person who planned to go on holiday to announce their day of departure to their neighbours long in advance. A *umkhwelo* or house party would then be organised for the weekend before their departure. African people from all around District Six would be invited. An admission fee was charged at the door, and inside, refreshments were sold. Requests for music encores were also paid for.

A record was kept of people who paid for anything at the house party.

What happened was that the person in whose honour the party was arranged would get a 24-page exercise book and ask a friend or member of the family to record all donations. For instance, if some people donated ten shillings or one pound their names would be written in the book. At the end of the party the guest of honour would be given the book to keep and to use for future reference so that they would know who donated what at the party and repay them whenever that person held a house party of his own.

The money that was collected would then be given to the guest of honour. It was a way of saying *hamba kahle* – go well! – to him or her. The whole arrangement was sort of a *stokvel*.

Because it was a *stokvel*, or *umgalelo*, as it is called in Xhosa, every person was given a chance to hold a house party. Not only was this a way to raise money, but it was also an important social event, a kind of entertainment.

In those days, it was common to hold such parties on Sunday afternoons. This was in order to make it possible for women to attend who "slept in" as domestic workers during the week. The ladies would wear their Sunday best, and so would their male friends.

The house parties would end at ten o'clock at night so that the women

Many "sleep in" domestics used to spend their off Sundays with friends in District Six. Miss Mahlanyana (left) regularly visited the Cele family in William Street. Many had their picture taken by a photo studio, and even though the name of the visitor on the right has been forgotten, the photograph is still cherished by the family she used to visit.

who were off duty on Sunday afternoons, would be in time for the last buses back to their "sleep in" places of work.

There were a few popular venues for these *stokvels*, but the most popular was No. 22 Stone Street.

At this address, which was a ten-minute's walk from Cross Street, lived Tat'uBhungane who had a very big room and a piano. He stayed alone because his family was in the country. The Black residents of District Six hired the room for one pound ten shillings, from one o'clock in the afternoon until ten in the evening. This was far cheaper than hiring the local halls at Primrose and Ayre Street, for instance. The person the party was given in honour of had to hire a pianist – *maskhanda*, as they were called in Xhosa. There were a few young men who were used as *maskhandas*.

The best income at such a party was from the bar. Much as the law did not allow the selling of liquor and the running of shebeens, this happened in a big way. If there was to be a house party, the shebeen queens would stock up beforehand with bottles and bottles of beer and brandy. Africans were not allowed to buy liquor over the counter, but that did not have much effect on the shebeen queens. They simply sent Coloured boys to buy it for them. The "carry-boys", or "mailers" as they were also sometimes known, charged a small sum for each bottle purchased – a tickey (three-pence), per bottle.

Every now and then a carry-boy tried to cheat on the shebeen queen by running away with the money given to him to pay for the liquor. It was not easy to trace such a skellum and of course it was impossible to report the theft to the police as the whole liquor business was illegal to start with. Because the carry-boys knew very well that they could not be reprimanded, they would vanish for a couple of days and then reappear and roam around as if nothing had happened.

THE SHEBEEN BUSINESS

The liquor was usually bought on Friday afternoons as the shebeen business was only good during the weekends. The Cross Street residents, like most other people in District Six, never consumed liquor during the week, and the police, who regulary raided the shebeens, chose Friday evenings to do so. Every Black child in District Six was aware of this and while playing in the streets on Fridays, they would be on the lookout for police vans. Whenever they spotted one, they would shout, "*Kubomvu! Kubomvu!*" – It's red! It's red! – red being the colour of danger. This was the signal to the residents that the police were on their way.

The police knew that they were being watched, so sometimes, instead of driving from Richmond Street into Cross Street, the obvious way to get there, they would drive down Dove Lane, and by the time the children saw them, it would be too late to shout, "*Kubomvu! Kubomvu!*" The ordinary residents of District Six never had telephones, but there was an excellent communications network operating throughout the area whenever there was a police raid. If the police raided in Cross Street, someone would quickly relay the message to Stuckeris Street to stash away any illegal stuff. From here, the news would be passed on to the "Strong Yard" in Roger Street, from where it went to Ashley, Caledon and William Street. By the time the *amaBhulu* got to these places, there would be no sign of liquor.

Sometimes, however, the police were too clever for the law-breakers. They would wear civvies, park their van far away and arrive on foot. Neither the children nor the older people would recognise them until they banged on the front or back door, as they always did. They never waited to be allowed in but forced the door open and moved from room to room, ransacking beds and wardrobes and leaving the place upside down. There was no respect for the people who lived there, they were only interested in the hidden liquor. Sometimes they did find a few bottles in a backyard, but nobody would own up, even if they threatened to arrest everybody, and in the end they left empty-handed because the owners' names were not written on the bottles.

There was one policeman who would always try to get us children to tell him where the liquor was. He was nicknamed "Rooikop" because he was a red head. But we would never tell, even though he would be walking right past the bottles safely tucked in stockings and hidden under the washing on the line.

One Monday morning, however, two of the residents, Sis'Nonto and Aunt Elsie who stayed at No. 24 Cross Street, were doing washing in the backyard and were chatting about how easily some of the children, especially the very young ones, could spill the beans.

"Do you know Lizzy from Ashley Street?" Sis'Nonto started the conversation.

"Of course I do, she sometimes sends me a few of her bottles to sell when business is not so good," replied Aunt Elsie.

"I met her at the butchery on Saturday. On our way out, she wanted to know if we had a raid on Friday."

"We didn't, did we?" asked Aunt Elsie.

"Of course not. We didn't have any raid on Friday and that's exactly what I told her. She looked surprised, though, so I had to convince her that I was home all day on Friday and there was no raid," said Sis'-Nonto.

"Why the surprise? There is no point in hiding a raid, is there?"

"Oh! no, there isn't." Sis'Nonto burst out laughing. "Alright, Elsie, this is what she told me. Do you know that she has a four-year-old son, Viwe?"

"Yes."

"Viwe was standing next to the table, waiting for his sandwich which Lizzy was preparing, when two White police officers walked in. Do you know what Viwe said when he saw the police?"

"No."

"'I know that these policemen are going to take my mother's liquor.'"

"*Suka wena,* Nonto, don't lie!" exclaimed Aunt Elsie.

"Not only that!" said Sis'Nonto. "He was staring directly at where the liquor was hidden."

"*Nkosi,* I can't believe this, what happened then?"

Sis'Nonto laughed before saying, "It's a blessing that Blacks don't blush, and even if they do, it doesn't show, otherwise Lizzy would have given herself away. She said she felt as hot as a stove, but she just remained rooted to her chair, trying to look as normal as possible. She softly called upon Viwe to shut up. *'Phuma, Viwe, phuma!'* – Get out, Viwe, get out! – she managed to say, and Viwe left the room.

"Children!" said Aunt Elsie, shaking her head.

"Yes, they tell a lot at Viwe's age. Anyway, the most fortunate thing was that the White police officers didn't understand Xhosa."

"What a relief! *Nkosi yam,* I hope Lizzy has learnt a lesson. She must make sure that either Viwe or the liquor is out of the house when the police arrive."

They both laughed.

ILLEGAL LIQUOR AND THE POLICE

When business got bad in District Six, the shebeen queens would boost their sales in the Langa shebeens where business was always flourishing because there were so many migrant workers who stayed in "bachelors' quarters" and whiled away their free time drinking.

The liquor was transported to Langa on Friday afternoon – not in bottles, but in a bicycle tube. Because it was awkward to carry glass bottles, a bicycle tube would be cut through and one end tied tightly with a thin wire. Once the brandy had been emptied into the tube, the remaining open end would be sealed with wire as well.

The person to take the stuff to Langa would tie the tube around her waist under her clothes. Off to Langa she would go, taking a bus at Sir Lowry Road on the outskirts of District Six and getting off at Mowbray. There she would catch a second bus to Langa. At Langa, the tube's contents would be emptied back into a bottle and sealed, ready for sale.

This method of liquor trafficking was practised for months and months without raising suspicion, until a detective from Langa police station got to know about it. From that moment he used to drive the police van to the Mowbray bus terminal and wait for the culprits. *"Ndiya kukrokrela,"* he would say confronting his victim – I suspect you. So the man was nicknamed Ndiyakukrokrela.

But the existence of Ndiyakukrokrela did not discourage the people from carrying on with their business. They just found out when he was on duty, and for the week that he worked the morning shift they avoided travelling to Langa during the day and chose the evening, and when he worked the afternoon shift, they travelled in the morning. Heaven knows who found out Ndiyakukrokrela's timetable, but whoever did, had accurate information.

The men living at No. 22 Cross Street were fond of keeping a few bottles of brandy to entertain friends at home. Friends would come all the way from BoKaap, a good half an hour's walk away, and spend the whole of Sunday afternoon chatting and drinking in District Six. The men used to share jokes, boasting about their experiences with the police or telling of incidents while they still lived in the country.

One joke they liked to share was that of Solomon Mpazi and Ernest Makupula who were confronted by three policemen on their way back from BoKaap late one Sunday afternoon.

"*Manene,* I never knew that Solomon was so stubborn," said Ernest to his friends. "You know, if it hadn't been for him, we would have been arrested."

"Tell us, Ernie, tell us what happened," one of the friends begged, still holding his empty glass.

"We were going up Hanover Street, just next to Maxim's Studio, when we were approached by three White policemen. Two were middle-aged and the third one was much younger."

"No, Ernie," Solomon interrupted. "They were all young. Don't be confused by the lines on their faces. That's caused by the way they pull their faces and the way they frown when they talk to Black people. That makes them look old! None of them could have been over forty."

The friends roared with laughter, while one was filling their empty glasses with beer. "If Sollie says so, then it's true," laughed Ernest. "Sollie must have seen them before I did because I saw him pull his hat down to just above his eyes when they came up and asked us why we were making noise on the street on a Sunday."

"Why did you do that, Sollie?" my father asked.

"Jimmy, I was preparing myself for *amaBhulu* because I saw them stop the van as soon as they spotted us, jump out and head in our direction. I knew they were coming to us and I didn't want them to see my eyes because they were red from the treat we'd had all afternoon."

At this point, Solomon took over from Ernest to relate the rest of the story.

"'Why are you making so much noise on the street on a Sunday, kaffirs?' the driver of the police van asked. I tilted my head so that I could look him straight in the eyes. I said, 'We're not making noise, we're talking.'

"'You're making noise, man,' he said, raising his voice.

"Then I replied, 'If our talking sounds like noise to you, then you do not know Black people.'"

The group laughed again, and Solomon, encouraged by the laughter, stood up and started imitating how the driver took his baton and pushed Solomon's hat backwards so that he could see his face properly.

"I held my hat with one hand and looked at the driver," continued Solomon. "He looked straight into my eyes and said, 'All I know about Black people is that they're kaffirs.'"

There was a slight pause, then Solomon sat down. There was no response from his friends this time, but all of them had the same expression on their faces, that of feeling undermined.

Solomon continued in a loud voice, "I looked at Ernie and he looked away. I got the message alright and I kept quiet."

"'You're drunk, kaffirs,' said the driver, spitting out the 'k'.

"'No, *baas*, we're not drunk,' Ernie said.

"'Alright then, if you're not, stand on one leg,' said the other policeman.

"We didn't move or say anything. Then the driver said, 'One leg, kaffirs!'

"I quickly moved towards a nearby pole, supported myself with one hand and lifted one foot.

"'Away from the pole!' shouted the third policeman.

"'Please show us what you mean,' I said.

"The second policeman lifted his one leg, but staggered. Then we both lifted ours and we both staggered.

"'There you are, you're drunk!' shouted the third policeman.

"'No, we're not,' I said.

"'Yes you are.'

"'Is your friend drunk?' I asked.

"'Are you trying to be smart, kaffir? How can he be drunk on duty?' intervened the driver.

"'Then we're also not drunk, because we were doing what your friend has shown us to do.'"

Solomon told the group how the argument had drawn the attention of some Coloured passersby. By now, a crowd was standing by, watching.

"I could see that the policemen were feeling uneasy. They later decided to ask for our 'pass' and we gave them our reference books. After scrutinising them, they threw them back at us and walked towards the van.

"'They're rude, aren't they?' a Coloured woman said.

"The driver turned back and stared at her," Solomon resumed. "At first I thought he was going to slap her face, but he was called back by his two colleagues. Just as he turned back and continued walking towards his colleagues, another bystander said, 'That one's very arrogant.'

"The driver did not look back this time, but we knew he'd heard the remark. The crowd started clapping their hands and later dispersed. We again set out on our way."

"That was very clever, Sollie," Ernest said, obviously very proud of his friend.

The whole group of listeners nodded their approval. Even Solomon looked satisfied and proud of himself, because he smiled back at the group and said, "That's why my old man named me Solomon."

Another incident that they liked to amuse themselves with was the one of Fuzani's friend and a sangoma.

Fuzani and a friend from Fort Beaufort had decided to go to Johannesburg to look for work. They were young bachelors who expected a lot from life, so their heads were full of ideas. One day they would come back to the countryside with a lot of money. They would be able to pay lobola, when the time came.

The friend got work as an induna on one of the mines and was better paid than the others, but still, he was not happy with what he was earning. At the mines, they had heard of a sangoma that had *muti* which could make people rich, so Fuzani's friend decided to go and see this sangoma.

This joke was even funnier because Fuzani who related the story stammered a lot, which got worse after two or three glasses of brandy.

"G-g-gentlemen, my friend was g-g-given a small b-b-b-bottle of medic-c-cine by the s-s-s-sangoma and was i-i-instructed not to open it until he was b-b-b-back at his home in the c-c-c-country. This happened on his last d-d-d-day at work j-j-just before he took his holiday. He p-p-put the b-b-bottle at the b-b-bottom of his suitcase and p-p-p-packed his clothes on top. He went b-b-b-back to Fort Beaufort by t-t-t-train and had to change at Cookhouse. He slept in the waiting room at the s-s-station because the next t-t-train to Fort Beaufort was the n-n-next morning."

The men were already smiling broadly.

"He p-p-put his s-s-suitcase underneath the b-b-b-bench he was s-s-s-sleeping on. The next morning, a b-b-big noise woke him. It was the train p-p-pulling into the station. He q-q-quickly got up and reached for his suitcase, b-b-but something very s-s-strange had happened. The s-s-suitcase was much much heavier! He p-p-pulled, but it would not move. He p-p-pulled again, but n-n-nothing happened.

"He was sure that it was his s-s-s-suitcase because there was the name t-t-tag with his name s-s-still attached to the handle. What's happening? he thought to himself. 'Oh no! Oh no!' he was remembering. 'It can't be! My word it can't be the s-s-s-sangoma, the s-s-stupid s-s-s-sangoma and his s-s-s-stupid b-b-b-bottle.'"

Everybody was blue with laughter, the narrator included.

"What happened to the s-s-s-suitcase, Oom Fuz?" imitated one friend.

"He t-t-t-took a quick decision. He left the s-s-s-suitcase where it was and b-b-b-boarded the train. He was so s-s-s-scared that he d-d-did not even look b-b-b-back."

"Ha! ha! ha!" laughed one friend. "Serve him right for being greedy."

Sometimes my father and his friends liked to argue about their age. What always amazed us children was that their age had nothing to do with their date of birth. Rather, it was related to the year they had come back from initiation school.

And age was important, because the youngest man would be sent on errands, like fetching more beer from the shebeen and pouring it out for the group. The pourer had to start with the oldest person present, and if he was not sure who was the oldest, he had to ask for guidance. Seniority had to be honoured and respect had to be shown at all times.

The *amaBhulu*, who seemed to know everything, were aware of these Sunday afternoon gatherings and regularly raided the popular spots on Sundays. If they did not find anything, they would resort to asking to see everyone's "pass".

One afternoon they raided Cross Street and found the group of friends chatting and drinking. The door of the upstairs room at No. 24 in which they were sitting was wide open because it was hot. The guy who was pouring the brandy had his back to the door. He was concentrating hard because everyone had to get exactly the same amount of liquor. But as he was measuring the brandy in a glass, something very unusual happened. People suddenly stopped talking. The young man did not notice, but whenever he offered a glass to someone, the man just shook his head. In the end, he must have sensed that something was wrong because he swung round. And there stood a big police officer with his colleagues, silently watching him.

The man nearly dropped dead with fear. It appeared that the police had heard a lot of noise coming from the room. Suspecting that there was drinking going on, they tiptoed upstairs and stopped at the door, keeping quiet and just watching. The drinkers were in a state of shock. They could hardly alert their friend who was happily filling the measuring glass – nor could they accept the brandy on offer.

The giant police officer started laughing very loudly and said, "Oh, kaffirs, you're drinking, neh?" Then, indicating the guy with the glass and bottle, he commanded, "Hey you! Drink all that brandy in that bottle."

The poor man could do nothing else but drink the remaining liquor, a little less than a quart. After he had emptied the bottle, the police left without making any arrests.

It was quiet in the room for some time. Only the coughing of the guy who had just gulped down the remaining brandy could be heard.

After they had made sure the police had gone, the friends crowded around their coughing friend, very concerned about the change of colour in his face.

He could not go to work the following three days because he had lost his voice.

The most upsetting part of the incident was that the man could have died from obeying the order of an irresponsible police officer. It was a miracle that he did not suffer permanent damage. If he had, I wonder if the officer would have taken responsibility.

Anyway, the whole episode would have been no big deal because the guy was African.

THE "DOMPAS" AND THE POLICE

Sometimes the police came only to raid those who did not have a "pass". The "dompas" was a booklet issued by the government to Africans, certifying their identity and granting them permission to stay in a particular area.

One Sunday afternoon, the police came across the usual Sunday gathering at Cross Street and asked to see everybody's pass. One of the residents – in fact, the father of Dennis and Lillian, my friend – who was Xhosa by birth but who "played Coloured", did not produce a "dompas". He presented an identity document. The officer looked at the document for a moment and threw it back in the man's face, hitting him on his left eye.

"Kaffir," the officer demanded, *"waar is jou dompas?"* – Where is your dompas?

The man, who used to be called Dan but who had changed his name to Daniels and used it as his surname, tried to explain to the officer that this was unfair, because he, Daniels, had already explained to him and his colleague that he did not have to carry a pass. He carried an identity document, because he was Coloured.

"Hey, don't play games with me," said the officer. "When we walked in you were all speaking kaffir-taal."

"Not me," said Dan. "I wasn't speaking Xhosa."

The officer stared at his neck and said, "You say you're Coloured?"

"Yes," replied Lillian's father.

"Can you then explain the two scratches on your neck? Kaffirs have that when they use *muti*."

Dan kept quiet and just stared at the officer.

"Talk man, do you still say that you are Coloured?"

"Yes," replied Lillian's father, with a frown. "I showed you my ID."

The other officer intervened by looking at the identity document, and when he had satisfied his curiosity, he pulled his colleague by the arm and they left.

"He can't do anything about it even if he's suspicious," said Lillian's father to his friends. "They made me Coloured the day they gave me that identity document. I can prove that in a court of law."

The other men did not say much, only one responded.

"You have to be so careful these days," Lillian's father said, looking around. "These Boere seem to know our life style. Did you hear the remark about the *umqaphulo*?" he asked, referring to the two scratches. "And what do they know about *umuti*?"

"They get the information from their Black colleagues," replied one man.

"We'll always do something to get round their laws," said Lillian's father. "It's not that I wanted to be Coloured, it's because of their job reservation laws! Coloureds have a much better chance in the workplace. An African won't get a job, even if he qualifies for it. Before he can get the job, it has to be offered to three Coloureds. It's only after they've all turned the job down that us Africans will be next in line." Lillian's father turned to the men on his left. "You know, as well as I do. With the pass laws that keep us out of the urban areas, there is little chance for a Black person to get a proper job and survive."

"Say that again," said another man in the group.

"Look at Mzwandile, for instance," explained Lillian's "Coloured" father.

"What about him?"

"Do you think that he ever dreamt of becoming a policeman?"

There was silence.

Mzwandile was a young man who had come from Qoboqobo to join his brother in Cape Town, with the aim of getting himself a job. This was not possible because Section 10 of the pass laws clearly stated that Blacks would be allowed to stay in an urban area, Cape Town in our case, only if they were "borners" – native inhabitants – of Cape Town. Or if they were in the service of one employer for a period of ten to fifteen years. Or if they were contract labourers who had married a Cape Town borner. Or if they had a visitation permit.

This permit was mainly given to married women whose husbands were contract labourers. The permit was valid for three months – enough time to give the woman a chance to conceive. After conception she had to return to the homelands.

If conception did not happen within three months, the permit was extended. Those days it was common for anybody who visited the Bantu Affairs Administration Board office in Langa to hear clerks calling forward couples who had this kind of permit and asking the husband if the wife had conceived.

64

Mzwandile did not qualify for a permit for any of the accepted reasons and fearing he would come across the police, his brother warned him not to walk around, especially in Hanover Street.

The young man could not avoid this, because most of the shops were in Hanover Street. So one day, he was arrested by the police. Mzwandile got a big fright. In the street he noticed another young man who he knew did not have a pass, so Mzwandile told the police about the other guy, hoping he would be let off lightly. So this guy, too, was arrested, and both were taken to Caledon Square police station and then to Roeland Street prison.

On the same day that these two were arrested I overheard my father saying, "Roeland Street prison is not the right place for young people." He was saying this to Hambani, Mzwandile's brother. "This is what I learnt from one of our drivers at work. I think you've met him. He is Bhayi, the tall chap who often visits here on weekends."

"Oh, you mean that one. Yes, I remember him, Tat'uMbele," said Hambani.

"He was arrested one Friday afternoon," my father continued. "For not having his 'dompas' with him. And he was taken to Roeland Street prison where he spent the whole weekend in a cell because he was only going to appear in court the next Monday morning.

"'Jimmy!' Bhayi said to me. 'That place is worse than hell, I'm telling you. Never ever allow a friend or relative to spend even one night in that place because one night seems like one year because of the pressure from both the wardens and the inmates. The treatment that you get from *amakhosi* because you are *mafikizolo* is unbearable. What is worse is you have to spend the whole night with old jailbirds in the same cell and they treat you like dirt. They mock you and they torture you because you're a newcomer. Hey, Jimmy! The worst torture is the bicycle.'"

"The bicycle! What do they do with a bicycle in a prison cell?" interrupted Hambani.

"*Hey wena,* Hambani! Listen. It's the most cruel thing I've ever heard. They let you lie on your back, put your feet up and one of the *amakhosi* is helped to stand on top of your feet and then you're instructed to move your legs, with him on top, as if you're pedalling a bicycle. You have to balance him, mind you! And make sure that you do it right because each time the *amakhosi* loses his balance and falls down, his friends come down on you. They kick you, and they beat you until they decide to stop. The more times the *amakhosi* falls off, the longer you're going to pedal your bicycle. By the time he gets off, your legs are as numb as rubber and your waist full of needles and pins."

"That's really cruel, Tat'uMbele. They behave like animals," Hambani agreed.

"Oh yes! That's how prison changes human beings. Please don't let your brother remain in prison," my father begged.

The Black residents of District Six were shocked by the arrest of Mzwandile and the other illegal man. After their release, the young men were advised to go elsewhere or back to Qoboqobo as the police were aware of their presence and would now increase their raids of Cross Street.

The second guy left for Johannesburg, but Mzwandile stayed on.

"The easiest way to get permission to stay in Cape Town is to apply for a job in the police force," one of Mzwandile's friends advised him. And that is exactly what Mzwandile did. His application was successful and he was sent for three months' training.

He came back a different person. He had lost a tremendous amount of weight, but all that mattered to him was that his permit was extended.

To us children, seeing the way the police handled our parents, we could never believe that Mzwandile would be an effective policeman. He was kind and very jocular by nature, and we could never associate his type of character with policing.

"It would really discredit me if my White colleagues would ever find you drinking or selling liquor in my presence," he would say to the Cross Street residents, who in return understood his position and always gave him the respect he deserved.

While Mzwandile was stationed at Windermere police station, he finally got a permanent permit. He could no longer be deported to Ciskei.

Mzwandile was the very first Black policeman in the area. This caused quite a stir. The Coloured neighbours were amazed when they saw him in police uniform for the first time. Because the pass laws did not affect them, they did not understand that Mzwandile had no choice. That he could actually maintain law and order in the area surprised them too. They did not believe it possible that a Black policeman could arrest a Coloured person. This had never happened before.

What I best remember about Mzwandile is how he always intervened and threatened to arrest the people who intimidated dogs in their mating season.

"What are you doing to the poor animals?" he would scream at the Coloured boys. "If you don't stop at once, I'll phone for the police van to come and pick you up."

The boys would immediately leave the dogs alone. But some of them would remark, *"Hy hou hom slim! Hy kan ons nie vang nie."* – He thinks he's clever, but he can't arrest us.

5

MAKING ENDS MEET

Talking about survival, the Black people of Cross Street had their way of making ends meet. As low as our parents' wages were, we never starved.

Many of our parents were employed at the fresh fruit and vegetable market, which is now at Epping. It was in Sir Lowry Road then, where the Good Hope Centre is today, about two kilometres from Cross Street. The people used to walk to work.

Every Friday afternoon we were sent to fetch fruit and vegetables. When we got to the market we would find the bags ready for us to take home, and not a single penny was spent.

The residents worked in various departments at the market. I am not sure whether as employees they were allowed to have the fruit and vegetables for free at the market, all I remember is that we visited various people in the various departments. Bhut'Gosa gave us fruit, for example, Tat'uGaba gave us cabbage and carrots, then from Bhut'Michael, we collected potatoes and onions.

Fruit and vegetables never appeared on anyone's grocery list. Everybody survived because of *ubuntu* – group solidarity. The deep sense of kinship controlled the social relationships between the Black inhabitants of District Six in the same way it did in the country.

The local grocery shops were owned by Indians and Muslims. These people knew exactly who they were serving, and even the poorest person in the community could afford to buy from them. Apart from having weekend specials, they used to offer stuff like fish oil, jam, sugar and coffee in quantities that one could buy for as cheap as two-pence. The shopkeeper would open a tin of jam and sell the contents by the tablespoon. The same went for the fish oil – for a tickey you could get a drinking glass of cooking oil.

This arrangement made life easy for everybody. Some of the shops even gave groceries on credit.

Talking of credit, selling on credit sometimes ended up in confrontation between the babie and his customers. One day, while I was in the shop, Esme, an eight-year-old Coloured girl, a neighbour, walked in with a credit book in her hand as well as a grocery list.

"Babie, Mummy has asked me to give you this," she said, handing over a grocery list. "And she asked me to tell babie that babie must enter it in the book, she'll pay on Friday."

"Oh no!" said the babie with a frown. "It's always pay on Friday. Come Friday, then I get a long story. Tell mummy to come herself," the Muslim shopkeeper said.

He then took my list and started packing my groceries in a middle-sized cardboard box, not even glancing in Esme's direction.

After totalling the price, he said, "That'll be one pound two shillings."

I took the money out of my pocket and handed it over.

"Basella, babie," I said. He took three sweets from a jar and put them on top of the groceries.

Esme was still standing and watching the babie. She stared at my sweets, looked at the babie and then asked, "Babie, where is my basella?"

"How can I give you basella, Esme? You didn't buy anything," replied the babie. "I told you to go back home and bring your mummy along with last week's payment, then I can give you basella."

Most Black families in District Six struggled to make ends meet, but some were better off. Sipho Cele, the fifth child of Michael and Olive Cele, one of the very few African children privileged enough to have had a tricycle in the early sixties, presently teaches at Mandela High School in Crossroads.

"Okay, babie, okay," she said and turned and walked out.

Having second thoughts, the babie called, "Esme! Come back!" Opening the big jar, he took out one sweet and gave it to her. Then he said, "I'll give you the other two when you come back with mummy."

Esme took the sweet with a smile and ran home.

Shoe, furniture and clothes stores were mostly owned by White people, stores like The Globe Furnishing Company, Shrands shoe store, and Waynicks, who sold school uniforms. The salesmen and -ladies, however, were Coloured.

Most of these shops took lay-byes. They allowed customers to choose what they wanted and pay only a percentage of the full amount. The customers could not take the items home, but the purchase would be set aside, and once the full amount had been paid off, it could be collected.

My mother made a lot of lay-byes for Christmas. She bought a suit, trousers, shirts, a pair of shoes, socks and underwear for my brother; for us girls she bought dresses, underwear, shoes and socks.

As early as June, she would start putting some things on lay-bye, and just before Christmas, she would pay for the lay-byes fully and then it would be time to go and fetch the items. This time always brought great joy, having to try on all those new clothes.

"Mama, will you still remember what you lay-byed?" Layton asked one day on the way to the shop.

"Of course, dear, my parcel has my name on. It's a matter of the saleslady fetching the parcel from the back and opening it, then I shall be able to remember all that's inside. Another thing – the items are written on my receipt, together with their prices."

When we reached the shop, we looked around and saw that quite a number of new items were on display. The old ones had been removed.

"Look, Mama!" I said. "Don't you think that the dress in pink over there is nicer than the one we chose?"

My mother looked at the dress and said, *"Hayi khona,* Nomvuyo, it doesn't compare with the green one. Look at the price! It's cheaper than the one we chose, which shows that it can't be better."

We walked inside. The saleslady recognised my mother at once and asked, "Are you coming for your lay-bye, mama?"

"Yes, my dear, I've brought the children along for fitting," my mother replied, taking out the receipt from her bag and handing it over to the saleslady.

The saleslady ushered us to the back room on the other side of the counter and promised, "I'll be with you in a minute." She reappeared quickly with a big parcel and said, "Here we are, mama," putting the parcel on the counter and opening it. She took out my light green dress and held it up for my mother to see. The bodice was made from embroidered material with small, button-like things that looked like pearls. It had a round lace collar and lace sleeves. The skirt was gathered, but made from a plain material. This material was also used to line the collar and the sleeves.

"Nomvuyo, do you still think that the pink dress in the window is prettier than this one?" my mother asked with a smile, her face full of satisfaction.

Before I could reply, a group of customers moved nearer and also admired it.

"It's beautiful!" one Coloured woman remarked. "Where can I find one like that for my daughter?"

"I'm sorry, lady, it's sold out. This one was put on lay-bye months ago."

"You will be the envy of all the girls in Cross Street," Layton said, patting me on the shoulder.

"Can I try it on, please, Mama?" I begged, feeling very excited and also happy to have an organised mother like her.

"Of course," the saleslady replied. "That's what you're here for."

We went into a cubicle and fitted all our new clothes, chatting happily. They all still fitted well. The saleslady wrapped them up again, handed the parcel to my mother and said, "Enjoy your Christmas attire, children," waving to us. We waved back and left the shop.

MAKING MONEY

Another way of keeping costs down was to buy dress materials and have our clothes made. There were a number of skilled Muslim dress-makers in the area.

My mother's favourite dress-maker was Mrs Adams from Chapel Street.

"She sure has a very neat finish," my mother would remark each time she brought back our dresses from Mrs Adams.

But one way of actually *making* money was to play the *fafi*, a type of illegal gambling game which was run by a Muslim guy in one of the shops in Hanover Street. Us children would be sent down to Hanover Street by the Cross Street residents who were punters to bet a certain number, and later we would be asked to go and find out the results. The numbers we had to bet on mostly came from the previous night's dreams or from an ordinary fancy. There was a belief, for instance, that if you dreamt of a dead man, you had to bet on number four. Number three represented water, and number eight stood for a pig or a fat person. This was how the dreams were interpreted.

For a bet you would be given a piece of paper by the Muslim guy with the number and the amount on it. You had to hang on to the piece of paper, because if you had bet on the winning number, you needed it to claim your money.

We knew that gambling was illegal, so we knew that we had to hide the pieces of paper from the police. Young as we were, we also realised that we could not go inside the shop if there was a policeman around.

We ate cheaply. At Castle Bridge was a butchery that sold offal. The offal arrived in the afternoon and was placed in a large tub near the door. After lunch, Black women started queuing for the offal because it was cheap and in demand. Like fish. So during the week, we ate tripe and trotters or fish, never red meat. That was too expensive and was served on weekends only. The fish was purchased at the fish market opposite the Star bioscope.

Sometimes over a weekend we had chicken. These chickens were tough, but plump and very tasty. They were bought from a man who worked on a farm. He charged five shillings per chicken and they were quite big. This man was related to Lillian's father Dan, the "Coloured" guy.

Orders were placed on Wednesdays and deliveries were made on Saturday mornings.

Madala, the man who worked on the farm, brought the live chickens to Cross Street. He would carry them in a sack on his back and on approaching he would call, *"Naz'iinkukhu!"* – Here are the chickens!

The residents who had placed orders with Dan responded to Madala's call by rushing to the stoep at No. 24, where the sales were done, to chose their chicken.

Some people also came to District Six to sell stolen goods.

They usually came to Cross Street on Saturday mornings. Instead of moving from house to house, they went to Dan's place at No. 24 because these sellers could communicate with him in Afrikaans. From there, Dan would move from room to room telling the residents that there was some *umgunyathi* – stolen goods – at his house going very cheaply. Lillian's father was always willing to organise for the sellers because he got something out of the deal.

The stolen goods were readily bought because they usually went for half the price they were sold for in the shops.

One day, two Coloured men arrived at No. 24 Cross Street by car. One of them went inside.

"What is it this time, Ronnie?" asked Dan.

"Suit-lengths, papa, and they're very cheap," replied Ronnie.

"Alright, bring them in while I organise the other neighbours," Dan said.

Ronnie went back to the car, took the car key from the driver and opened the boot. They each carried a big box into Dan's house. Solomon, my father Jimmy, Ernest and Radebe were already in Dan's house when Ronnie and his friend entered with the goods.

When Ronnie opened the first box, everybody moved forward to feel the texture of the material. They all agreed that it was good stuff.

"How much is this one?" asked Solomon, holding up one of the suit-lengths.

"They all go for ten shillings, papa," said Ronnie, rubbing his hands.

"Give me the bottom one, Sollie," my father said.

"Take two, Jimmy, this is real *mgunyathi*. Where will you ever get this stuff for ten shillings again?" Solomon advised.

"Alright, let me choose another one," my father agreed.

After making his choice, he took out of his pocket a one-pound note and gave it to Ronnie, and left. Most of the residents decided to buy the suit-lengths and the boxes were empty within a short time. After the sale, Ronnie gave Dan his tip, went back to the car and drove away.

We were all very excited. My father had bought two of the suit-lengths! But he was clever enough to take them to a tailor the very same day.

On the following day a police van stopped in front of our building. My mother was standing at the window and when she saw the van, she remained where she was and watched.

The police came out and opened the back door. Out came Ronnie and his friends.

"Mbele!" my mother called out to my father. "It's the police and the two Coloured men who were selling suit-lengths yesterday."

"*Hayi bo!* Are they coming in?" my father asked.

"I'm not sure," my mother said, moving away from the window.

Just then, my brother Layton came up the stairs.

"Where are the police?" my father asked him.

"They have gone into No. 24, Tata, into Bhut"Dan's house," he replied.

"Where are my reading glasses?" my father asked.

He opened the wardrobe, took the glasses, sat down in his armchair and pretended to be reading the newspaper.

It was quiet for a while, then we heard footsteps. They were coming up the stairs.

My father indicated to my mother to look busy. She stood at the stove and started to stir the pot.

The door flew open and Ronnie was thrown inside.

"Do you know this one?" the police asked Ronnie. Not waiting for him to reply, the police confronted my father.

"Papa, where are the suit-lengths?"

"Which suit-lengths?" my father asked, looking very cool.

The police went straight to the wardrobe, opened it and looked, but they could not find anything.

They left our room and banged on the door next to ours. It was locked, the owner was away. They went downstairs again.

We all went to the window. There was Sollie, Radebe and Dan getting in at the back of the van, guilt written all over their faces.

The suit-lengths were apparently stolen from a factory in Woodstock, where the two guys were employed. Information had leaked out who the culprits were. They were arrested and got a couple of punches from the police, which made them say, "*Wag, my baas, ons sal julle wys waar ons die goed verkoop het.*" – Wait, boss, we'll show you where we sold the stuff.

There was of course a lot of foul play in the back-door business. One man, Mabhunu from Ashley Street, thought that he was buying a bag of sugar. In fact, the sellers who had opened the bag for him to see, and even insisted that he taste it, convinced him it was sugar he was buying. But the next day his wife said, "Come and have a look what is at the bottom of your bag of sugar."

The man poured the sugar from the bag and discovered that the bottom part of the bag was filled with sand! Just a thin layer of sugar was spread on top. How clever! There was no way the poor man could recover his money because the cheat had disappeared into thin air.

6

KEEPING TRADITIONAL VALUES ALIVE

Not all the Black residents of District Six lived with their families. Some had left their wives and children in the country and came as contract labourers, renting rooms as bachelors. This is why a few always returned to the country during the festive season. It was time to visit their wives and children.

But there were some men who stayed in Cape Town for years and years without thinking of getting back to their families. In some cases, they didn't even send sufficient maintenance money to their wife and children. Instead, a number of them found themselves a *masihlalisane* – a common-law wife – and started making another family in Cape Town. This was strongly discouraged by the elderly people, though they knew deep down that the pass laws were the cause of the problem.

The elders, the *abantu abadala*, were a link between the family in the country and the men in the city who were shirking their responsibilities. If they discovered somebody was neglecting his duties, a meeting would be arranged and the person summoned to appear before a sort of disciplinary committee.

Six of the most elderly residents of Cross Street formed our disciplinary committee. Solomon Mpazi, who lived at No. 24, was the chairman and the other members were Ernest Makupula, Philemon Ngele, my father Jameson Ngcelwane, Deki Njobe and Albert Makhabane. Cases were reported to Solomon, who would then call a meeting of the committee – *ibhunga* – at his house, usually on a weekday evening or on a Saturday afternoon. Before summoning the accused, Solomon would always first discuss the matter with his committee.

The hearing was usually short and simple.

"There is a letter here we would like you to read to us," the chairman would begin, handing the letter to the accused.

After the letter had been read out, usually with a lot of pauses in between, the chairman would continue, "Can we accept what you are being accused of as true and correct?"

Members of the St Columba's Anglican chapel choir, 1959. Dressed in black-and-white uniforms, they used to sing during the church service only, not at night concerts as well, like the Methodist choir. Mrs Mamiya Makhabana, 2nd row, 2nd from left, lived at No. 26 Cross Street. Her husband Albert was not a member of the choir but of the *ibhunga* – the street disciplinary committee.

Silence.

"Well, seeing that you are not denying the allegation, we assume that it is hundred per cent true. May we then have your pay slip so that we may be able to show you what a man with a family is supposed to do?"

This of course would be said with a lot of sarcasm.

At this stage no excuse would be accommodated. A decision would be taken on how much money was to be posted to the man's wife.

"Do you think your family live on *amatye* – stones? Or do they perhaps have the magic to change *amatye* into money? *Usisidenge!* – You are a fool! If you are not careful, your in-laws will take their daughter back. You let her starve any longer, and you will be a nobody! How can you disgrace your father like this!"

After these strong words, two men would be elected to monitor the process and later report back to the committee. Decisions taken by the committee were seen as binding and no one dared ignore them.

I still remember an incident that involved a guy whose clan name was Mbele. He drank a lot, and did so on a daily basis. He could hardly buy clothes for himself, let alone send money to his family.

Various residents talked to him about his unacceptable behaviour, but there was no improvement. In the end, it was decided that he would have to be escorted back to Tsolo in Transkei where he came from. He had lost his job through drinking, and that had made things worse. With his back-pay he had bought a lot of booze and had made friends with other loafers in the area.

The residents collected money for his train fare and a "go-well" house party was arranged. People from as far as Langa were invited. The turnout was very good because the invitees had been told about the intended escorting. Everybody was concerned about this guy because he had lately reached the drinking level of sleeping on the streets. This was a disgrace, and especially the elders were very upset. They argued that no Black man who had gone to initiation school could sink that low – no, he *had* to go home.

Dudulele was told about the *ukutrokwa* – escorting – on the day of his departure. The train ticket had been purchased and the suitcases were packed with clothes donated by the residents. One of the elders from Tsolo, Naphtalie Mabandla, advised him, "Dudulele Mbele, I've been asked by amaBhele and the other residents of Cross Street to tell you that we have decided to deport you back home today because of your behaviour."

Dudulele stared at him for a moment, not believing what he was hearing.

"*Hayi khona,* you can't do that to me. You can't treat me like that! I'm not a child!" Dudulele protested, standing up.

"But you are behaving like a child, Dudulele!" Naphtalie said, raising his voice. "How many times have we tried to talk to you?"

Dudulele opened the door, trying to get out as fast as he could.

"Dudulele! Dudulele!" Naphtalie called out. This was enough to send the men who were waiting in a room next door rushing over.

"Catch him! He's running away!" Njobe shouted.

Dan and Ngele caught him on the stairs and pushed him back inside the room.

"*Liphi igqudu?* – Where is the knobkierie? – He's resisting!" Ngele said.

One of the residents threw a knobkierie at Ngele who in turn hit Dudulele on the head with it.

"Tie his hands behind his back, he's getting out of hand!" some residents suggested.

But the knobkierie had done its job. It had brought back Dudulele's senses. He realised that the residents were serious and decided to conform.

The people started to sing –

Nkosi uzusikelele amaBhele, amaBhele
Kulo lonk'ixesha labo, lokuhlal'emhlabeni...
God bless the Mbele clan, the Mbele clan,
as long as they live on this earth ...

This song was composed by my mother specially for the Mbele clan because she had noticed that they liked to sing at their Sunday afternoon gatherings. My mother (who was not a Mbele, though my father was) had taken the rather sad tune from a song she sang at school, but the words she composed herself.

Now they sang the song as a farewell song. Dudulele had a beautiful voice and took over, leading the group. The people, a few women in particular, became emotional as the song went on and on. The men stood with their heads bowed and their hands crossed in front of them as they sang.

Tears were rolling down Dudulele's cheeks but he kept on singing.

Two of the women, Mrs Njobe and Makupula's wife, covered their faces with their aprons. My mother cried openly, sobbing softly as she leaned against the wall.

Finally, Dudulele stopped singing. He thanked the residents for their concern and all they had done for him.

"MaBhele, I'm deeply moved by what you've done for me today," he started. "Yes, I did not want to accept the idea of *ukutrokwa* at first, but now I can see that you're doing this because you couldn't watch my behaviour deteriorating any longer. I was born and brought up in Tsolo, therefore Tsolo is my home. If you send me to Tsolo, you do so because you have hope that things will get better. I hope they will maBhele!"

He paused for a moment and continued, "I'm so ashamed, so very ashamed of myself, maBhele. Look at me! Just look at me. Even if you were to slaughter me and throw me to the dogs, I'm sure they would sniff and walk away."

After saying this he began to cry, touching everybody's heart. He wiped his face with a handkerchief, given to him by Njobe. "I'm willing to go home, there's no need to tie me up. You have shown your love for me and I will always appreciate your gesture."

Then the group left for the station.

That was the last we saw of Dudulele. He died in Tsolo two years later.

TO DO AND DIE, AND NOT TO REASON WHY

We children, too, had rules to follow. Rules like going on errands for every neighbour that asked you to; accepting something from an adult with both hands, and avoiding the use of obscene language. Any adult who caught a child doing something wrong had a duty to perform – that of punishing the child on the spot and later reporting the incident to the parents.

There was this belief that punishment immediately after an offence had more meaning than shelving it for later. It also served to suppress a habit from forming, they believed. So children dared not tell their parents when one of the neighbours had reproved them, fearing that they would have to face another punishment. The adults formed a united front when it came to the disciplining of children. Our parents were very strict indeed. They never took any nonsense from the youth. It was our lot to do and die, and not to reason why.

One Saturday morning, round about eleven o'clock, Gidi, Tat'uMakupula's son, was sent by his father to a friend in Woodstock, to go and collect some money. This money was going to be used to pay the rent as Abdullah was coming to collect rent that afternoon. Gidi, of course, did not know this, and because he had already made plans with his friends to go to the Avalon cinema that afternoon and it was getting late, he decided to go from Woodstock straight to the cinema.

At about two o'clock, his father began to panic. "What could have happened to Gidi? It's going on for two o'clock and he's not back yet," he said to his wife.

"Don't worry yourself. I'm sure he'll be back before Abdullah comes for the rent," she said, trying to calm him.

Unfortunately, Gidi was not back in time. When Abdullah arrived, Tat'-uMakupula could not pay his rent, so he had to doublepay the following month. This worried him a lot because all the tenants were faithful and reliable to Abdullah, and besides, Tat'uMakupula did not want to fall behind with his rent.

Gidi came home around five-thirty, as cool as a cucumber.

"What has taken you so long?" his father asked. "I hope you've not lost the money."

"Oh no, Tata," replied Gidi, taking the money out of his pocket. "I was going to be late for the movies, so I decided to go straight to the Avalon."

He had hardly finished, when the old man took one of his shoes and threw it at the boy, but missed. Tat'uMakupula moved swiftly towards Gidi, who turned and headed for the door. Unfortunately, he tripped over a chair and was caught by the collar of his shirt.

"I'm going to teach you that first things come first," said Tat'uMaku-pula, pulling the boy up on his two feet, trembling with fury.

His wife quickly ran outside and screamed for help. Radebe, the next-door neighbour, came running in and tried to separate the two, but in vain. Tat'uMakupula was now punching Gidi on his face and back with his fists.

"Stop! Makupula, stop!" cried Solomon as he rushed in. "You're too angry to handle this." He grabbed the old man while Radebe tried to free the boy. They were finally separated, but Radebe still held Gidi by the arm.

"Alright," said Solomon, "let's tie the boy to this chair so that he does-n't get away. And you must come with me," he said, pulling Gidi's father by the arm. They both went outside, leaving Radebe with the boy.

"What's happening?" asked two other neighbours whose attention had been drawn by the noise.

"Go inside and help Radebe tie up that boy," instructed Solomon. "After that you can join us in my room," he said. The three men made sure that Gidi was well tied before they joined the others in Solomon's room.

After Tat'uMakupula had related the whole incident, they all agreed: for punishment, Gidi should be left tied up. So Gidi was left with his mother in the room. He complained to her that the ropes were too tight, begging her to loosen them.

"You know I cannot do what you're asking," said his mother in an authoritative way.

"I'm not asking you to free me, Mama. Just loosen the ropes, they're hurting me," he begged.

"Forget it," she replied.

Seeing that his mother was not prepared to help him, Gidi tried to free his hands, only to make matters worse. The ropes were eating into his flesh. By now, his right eye was swollen and his hands were also swelling slowly.

There came a knock at the door. It was Jibi, a neighbour, looking for Gidi's father.

"Please, Tat'uJibi, untie me, these ropes are eating into my flesh," Gidi begged.

Jibi, who was a bit drunk, took a look at Gidi's hands. Seeing how swollen they were, he asked, "Who tied this poor boy this way? This is dangerous. It's hampering his blood circulation."

"No, Tat'uJibi, don't ever think of untying Gidi, you'll be in trouble," replied Gidi's mother.

"But mama, I can't leave him like this," replied Jibi and he began to untie him, taking his time because of his lack of balance.

Gidi was only too happy to be free. He left the room quickly, rubbing his hands.

"Don't worry, mama, I'll tell Makupula myself that I untied the boy," said Jibi.

"You better do that quickly, you'll find them in Solomon's room," advised Gidi's mother.

Jibi left the room and went upstairs. There he found the men chatting and drinking beer as if nothing had happened.

"May I have your attention, Makupula?" Jibi said, raising his hands. "I've come to tell you that …"

"Shut up, Jibi, and sit down before you fall on us," said Solomon jokingly.

After he had sat down, Solomon asked, "What have you come to tell us, Jibi?"

"That I've untied the boy."

There was a long silence in the room, everybody staring at Jibi. Then he continued, "If it weren't for me, that boy could easily have died. His hands and eye were already swollen."

"Enough, Jibi, enough! Before you say anything further, this group is charging you a bottle of brandy."

"Yes, *siyakudla*, Jibi. We're fining you for not behaving like a man!"

A meeting of the *ibhunga* was also called when a man hit his wife. This, fortunately, rarely happened, but when it did happen, the couple would be summoned by Solomon. The husband, guilty or not, would be fined a bottle of brandy for disturbing the peace. He would be excluded from drinking from this bottle, which was a sign of punishment, while the other men enjoyed it. Since the group structure was so important to everybody, the offender would conform fully to its laws.

Amongst the residents of Cross Street was an old woman whom we all called Gogo – Grandmother. She was very kind and strong and was liked by everybody. At the age of sixty, she was still employed as a domestic servant. She had been working for a White family for many years and "slept in", but she was given a half day off on Thursdays to attend the women's *Umanyano* – Christian union – at St Columbus because she was Anglican. Every Thursday Gogo wore her *Umanyano* uniform – a black skirt, black shoes, purple blouse with a white collar, and a black velvet hat.

In her uniform, Gogo, looked much younger than her sixty years.

When we sometimes asked my mother why Gogo did not have a family and was all by herself at that age, Mama would say, "All the residents of Cross Street are Gogo's family. So even if she has no children of her own, she is not lonely."

It was true. Everybody was always willing to help Gogo out. I also had a duty to perform for her.

Gogo never went to school so she could neither read nor write. It was my duty every second Thursday of the month to write her letters. She spoke some Afrikaans because she grew up on a White man's farm in Lusikisiki and liked to mix her Xhosa and her Afrikaans. "Don't think you're *slim!*" she would say when someone was showing off.

Gogo was a very organised old woman and very neat and she would have her stationery ready for me when I arrived. She would begin dictating as soon as I had sat down. But I had a problem with Gogo's dictation, because she said the same thing over and over again. The first part of the letter would be a series of questions, asking after the wellbeing of nearly half of the population of the village she came from. The letter would be structured this way: How is Tshawe? Is he still well? How is maRadebe? Is she still attending the women's *Umanyano*?, and so on.

Sometimes Gogo would forget the names and ask me to remind her. How on earth could I know, I who had never been to the village in the first place?

In the end, I decided to summarise the messages. But this was not easy because at a certain point, Gogo would ask me to read to her what I had written, and she easily picked up that I had left out some of the messages, and the names. The only way to get around this problem was to tell her, "Gogo, the names will be added at the bottom."

Gogo was of great assistance to the young mothers in our street. Just about all the babies who suffered from sleeplessness or wind were taken to her for treatment. She had a vast number of small bottles of medicine which she mixed and rubbed the babies with. The rubbing helped a lot and the residents believed that Gogo had magic hands. To me, this was quite strange as she never had children of her own.

Gogo also acted as a social worker to young couples with domestic problems. She would advise the young women who confided in her how to treat their husbands.

"Gogo, I think my husband's involved with another woman," maLimakwe confided to Gogo one day.

"Did he say so?" Gogo responded.

"Hayi khona, Gogo, men never tell. It's only that he comes home late, say, twice or three times in the week."

"Has he explained why?" Gogo asked.

"No, and that's what makes me suspicious."

"Have you asked him about his latecoming?"

"Not yet, that's why I've come to you."

"If he hasn't said anything, it's obvious that he doesn't want you to know because it's not important. Give him time, he'll tell you, but you mustn't ask him anything, do you hear me?"

"Alright, Gogo, if you say so."

"That's a good girl," Gogo said with a smile, patting maLimakwe on the shoulder.

And that was the end of maLimakwe's marital problems.

Because Gogo could not read or write, she never banked her money. Instead she gave it to her "home-boy", a fellow who came from the same home town as she, and whom she trusted. Nyawuza kept a record of Gogo's money in a 24-page exercise book. I knew about the book because Gogo would take it out from time to time and ask me to read the last entry to her. I never heard her querying the entries and so I thought that all was well.

Of course, all *was* well with the entries. It was when the time came for Gogo to leave Cape Town that there was a problem. The man was nowhere to be found. Gogo had trusted a crook.

The old woman cried bitterly when she learnt that her home-boy had resigned from his work some time before and had left Cape Town for good.

"Can you believe this? Nyawuza is nowhere to be found. He's gone with all my money. My life-time savings! What shall I do?" she sobbed.

People could not believe that such a dignified man could stoop so low. Everybody sympathised with the old lady. Something had to be done. One of the residents was asked to accompany Gogo to the White family for whom she had worked and tell them what had happened. Gogo's employer was sympathetic enough to offer her a train ticket to Transkei, and the residents organised a house party, an *umkhwelo*.

I asked my mother to bake Gogo a raisin loaf, which was her favourite, as provision on her journey home. The women's *Umanyano* also assisted Gogo with a few items and some cash.

Gogo was accompanied to the station by some of the residents from Cross Street. They carried her luggage, while she clutched her handbag in one hand and a white handkerchief in the other. After the little group had walked a little distance, Gogo looked back at us and called, "Farewell, dear children, may God bless you. *Enkosi,* my children, thank you," and she waved goodbye with her white handkerchief.

We waved back and shouted, *"Hamba kahle,* Gogo, go well," until she vanished down Richmond Street.

It was sad to me to see her go this way, when she thought she had made other plans for this day.

7

DANGER AFTER DARK

To the Black residents of District Six, weekends meant visiting friends. Apart from visiting one another around the neighbourhood, they also visited friends in the township. It was common in those days to see people travelling to Langa or Nyanga by bus or by train, and it was the custom for the residents of Cross Street to check on each other before they went to bed in the evening. It was not always safe to walk in Hanover Street late

Mbijana Nokhubeka, flanked by two friends, on his way to town. When I was young, African men liked to wear hats – and robbers used to be tempted to steal them! Roving photographers working for Movie Snaps specialised in "snapping" people in the streets of Cape Town.

My parents James and Elizabeth Ngcelwane. My father is wearing his favourite Battersby hat and my mother her Sunday best. The picture was taken as a keepsake after my father came from hospital where he was treated for a serious illness. Every Sunday my parents would attend the Methodist church in Chapel Street dressed in this fashion. Most formal photographs of District Six residents were taken either by Maxims Studio, like this one, or by Van Kalker.

at night, especially if you had to go past the Seven Steps, and residents constantly reminded one another of the risk involved in coming back late.

Black men liked to wear hats those days. My father's favourite was a Battersby, and his favourite colour was grey. Thieves also liked hats those days, and people who returned late were sometimes robbed of their hats.

One Sunday evening as Philemon Ngele was going past the Seven Steps, a Coloured guy called, "Papa, papa, cigarette please." The man was standing with a group of young men.

"I'm sorry, I don't smoke."

"Do you perhaps have one shilling for me?" the guy insisted.

Philemon did not reply this time. He just walked faster. The group started stamping their feet on the ground. The sound of loud footsteps

85

sent Philemon running. Two members of the group immediately chased after him and caught up with him next to The Globe Furnishing Company. One grabbed his hat and the other his left arm – to get his wrist watch. Fortunately at that moment a car with lights on came down Clifton Street and the two men let him go and ran away. His watch was still on Philemon's arm, but he had lost his hat!

Robberies were reported to the disciplinary committee by the victims and discussed at great length, and the spots where the robbers hung out were avoided. The Seven Steps leading off Hanover Street was the most notorious place for robberies. My father used to say that you are never safe until you have passed the Seven Steps.

"If you go past the Seven Steps in the evening without being harassed," he always said, "then you must know your ancestors are with you."

To avoid this place, the residents who travelled back from Langa by bus got off at Sir Lowry Road instead of Castle Bridge near the public toilets. From there they would walk up Stuckeris Street as far as Hanover Street, cross and continue up Richmond to Cross Street. This was not the shortest route, but it was the safest way after dark.

Once Mzwandile's brother, who was asthmatic, and Themba Memani, a young, energetic sportsman, came home from Langa by this route. It was Saturday and they caught a double-decker bus from Mowbray into town. On the lower deck, near the door of the bus, two White policemen were standing. At the Sir Lowry Road bus stop, Themba and his friend rang the bell and descended from the upper deck. The police, as usual, harassed them.

"*Maak gou*, kaffirs! Hurry up!"

The two did not argue but quickly got off the bus. Only when it had moved a few yards away, they started swearing at the police.

"*Wat sê julle*, kaffirs?" one policeman demanded.

"You heard, you white pig," Themba replied.

That was enough. The two policemen jumped off the bus and went for them.

"Wait for me, Themba! *Sukudishiya!* – Don't leave me behind!" shouted Mzwandile's brother.

"*Baleka, man!* Run, man! *Afikile amaBhulu*. The *Boere* are coming!" Themba called back.

Themba was faster than his friend, but Mzwandile's brother tried to keep up with him. He knew that if the police caught him, he would pay for the sins of his friend as well. As they could never catch Themba, who ran like the wind, Mzwandile's brother vowed to himself that they would not catch him either.

The poor fellow was overtaxing himself. He wheezed and panted but still could not shake off the two policemen. As the road went uphill, the police drew nearer. Just when they were about to grab hold of him, a group of Coloured men started shouting, "Hey! *Los hom, los hom uit!* Leave him alone!"

The police, sensing trouble, turned back.

When they reached Cross Street, Mzwandile's brother and Themba Memani were so tired that they could hardly talk. Only later did they tell the story and praise the Coloured men for saving their skins.

Bhenya, another resident, was, however, less fortunate. It was the same weekend, and he had gone to BoKaap on foot to visit friends. Because he knew that he would be coming back late and would be passing the Seven Steps, he had taken along his sjambok as protection. On his way back, Bhenya saw a group of young men sitting on the Seven Steps, as he had feared. He decided to carry on regardless.

When he drew nearer, one of the skollies got up.

"*Het djy 'n metsjie?* Do you have a match?" he asked.

This, of course, was an old trick. As soon as Bhenya put his hand in his pocket for the match, the man grabbed the sjambok and started whipping him.

At first, Bhenya faced his opponent as if he was going to fight back.

"*Slaan hom!* Beat him!" encouraged the skollie's friends.

The skollie got in a few good swipes while Bhenya tried to get hold of the whip. The skollie only pushed him away and whipped harder. Bhenya could not stand the pain. He turned around and started running. The group of young men roared with laughter.

"*Ja hom! Ja hom!* Chase him! Chase him!" they shouted.

Bhenya ran for his life all the way back home. Whoever had used his own sjambok on him had done a good job because his back was covered with nasty purple welts.

Word about Bhenya's whipping immediately went round District Six. To some, it was a joke because Bhenya had been warned time and again by his relatives not to carry the sjambok around.

"If you have to carry something, let it be a walking stick rather," they had begged him. "A sjambok is too dangerous."

Bhenya had ignored the advice and paid the price.

A NASTY SURPRISE

A lot of pickpocketing also took place on the buses, especially on Fridays. Residents were robbed of their wrist-watches, money and hats. Some even lost their total weekly wages this way.

A group of people, the pickpockets, would stand at the exit of the bus and as the passengers moved past them on their way out, they would empty their pockets, jump off the bus and disappear.

Sometimes the bus conductor intervened, but this was not easy when the bus was full. The pickpockets often refused to pay the bus fare, because, they said, they were in actual fact only travelling along to do their work. If an argument developed, the bus conductor often lost out and might even get stabbed.

One Friday, during peak hour, Gilbert, who lived in Tyne Street, was coming back from work in the city. He boarded the Hanover Street bus near the station. During the week he walked home, but taking the bus was his Friday routine. On Fridays he also carried a knife in his pocket.

"I have seen so many robberies on the bus that I made up my mind long ago to carry a knife when I go to work on Fridays," Gilbert explained when he later told us the story.

"I always hoped that one of those guys would try to pick my pocket. I'd teach those skollies a thing or two!"

Gilbert's wish came true that Friday. As he came down from the upper deck, he saw the group standing at the exit. He excused himself so he could pass, but nobody moved. This was their strategy, he knew, so he slipped his pocket knife into his hand and waited, ready.

The next moment he felt something touching the back pocket of his trousers and he grabbed. He got hold of someone's hand, quickly turned round and stabbed the pickpocket's wrist. "You bastard, what do you think you're doing?" he asked between clenched teeth.

"*Ek het niks gedoen nie!*" – I did nothing! – the pickpocket screamed.

"I'm going to show you something today," Gilbert said, pulling the open knife hard across the man's wrist.

"Leave me!" the pickpocketer cried out, trying to free his hand.

Some women passengers at the door started screaming.

"Where's the conductor? Call him! Will someone call the conductor please!" one woman shouted.

There was chaos at the exit because passengers were now pushing their way further inside the bus, away from the exit, trying to get back to their seats.

"*Eina, jou bliksem!*" the guy yelled, and his friends, sensing that there was trouble, jumped off the bus.

My mother was so shocked when Gilbert came to this part of the story that she begged him not to continue. But Gilbert carried on.

"I didn't get off at my usual bus stop next to Shrands shoe store. I jumped off at the corner of Muir Street instead, to mislead them," he boasted.

For once the pickpockets were beaten at their own game and Gilbert came back home a happy man.

8

THE AFRICAN MILLS BROTHERS

In the early 1950s, there was a musical group in District Six called the Flames. They were under the management of Gordon Koboka of Tyne Street. After some time, some of the vocalists decided to break away because they were not satisfied with the manager. They formed a new group and called themselves the African Mills Brothers.

The African Mills Brothers were deeply inspired by the music of the Mills Brothers of the United States, and in 1953 they started to roll.

Everybody knew and loved the African Mills Brothers, here posing in modern outfits. The only member of the group still alive today is Ndokosi Maqungo, 2nd from left, who is a minister in the Moravian church in NY 15 Guguletu.

The African Mills Brothers used to change their attire during shows. Traditional Xhosa songs – which always greatly excited the Black audiences – were performed in these outfits.

Their manager, Benwell Mandindi, was a close friend of "Oom Dan", a promoter who lived in Dickson Street in BoKaap. Oom Dan was an expert at organising shows and afternoon spends in District Six.

"Ben, I have a job for your boys," Oom Dan said every time he approached Benwell.

"Boys, I had a visit from Oom Dan."

Every time Benwell said this, it brought excitement to the vocalists – Andy Masiba, the leading voice, Cyril Mandindi, Alfred Mandindi, Thami Mcosana, Rueben Mdlalo, Zola Maqungo, and Ndokosi Maqungo, the last male singer to join the group.

Later that same year, the men decided to rope in Irene Bachelor, a good soprano soloist, who was very popular in the area because of her repeated success in the Black Miss Cape Town beauty pageant. Not only did she have a beautiful face, she also swung her body gracefully to the backing music provided by the vocalists.

"Encore! Encore!" the audience would roar during a concert, jumping up on their seats, especially at the rendition of the extremely popular

Irene Bachelor, a good soprano who repeatedly won the Black Miss Cape Town beauty pageant, often sang with the African Mills Brothers. All of them residents of District Six, they were popular in and outside the area.

"Wayeshilo, watsh'umama wath'uma mandibuyel'ekhaya" ("Mum said I should come back home"), which was always a show-stopper.

The African Mills Brothers loved their music and because of their generosity were loved in turn by all District Six residents. They never charged a fee when they were requested to perform in a show organised by Black people, so they regularly appeared free of charge at the Black Miss Cape Town beauty pageant.

They also sang at Sunday afternoon spends at the Clyde and the Ayre Street halls, and at fund-raising concerts organised by the Chapel Street school and the Methodist church. But since they were known throughout Cape Town, they were sometimes invited to sing at the Drill Hall and the City Hall. For these occasions of course they charged a fee.

Andy Masiba and his boys were real professionals. They performed in black trousers, off-white jackets, white shirts and black bow ties. Sometimes they preferred white trousers and floral shirts, or if the occasion called for it, traditional wear. These outfits they purchased out of their own pockets, because there were no sponsors for Black performing artists those days.

My eldest sister, Nombulelo, was a close friend of Joy, the Reverend Zwane's daughter. She and some other friends used to help Joy make tea and serve scones at the all-night concerts organised by the Methodist church in Chapel Street. Such a concert would start at eight o'clock on Saturday evening and end at six the following morning. Because members of the church choir rendered most of the music, they had to be served tea and scones right through the night to keep them going.

My father always gave Nombulelo permission to attend the concerts, even though she would only be coming home the next morning, because it was a service she was giving.

One Saturday evening Nompumelelo accompanied her. Round about three o'clock, in the early hours of the next morning, there was a knock on our front door. My father was hesitant to open the door because it was still too early for the girls to be expected back.

From where I was sleeping in the corner, I heard my mother whisper something to him.

"Who is it? Who is at the door?" my father asked at last, standing close to the door.

"It's us, Tata," came Nombulelo's answer.

My father, on recognising my sister's voice, quickly opened the door. And there stood my two sisters, one looking very cross and the other very drowsy.

"What's wrong, Nombulelo? Why have you come back so early?" my father asked, very concerned.

Nombulelo walked past him to my mother, who was still in bed. "You see, Mama," she complained. "I told you that Nompumelelo's too young to attend night concerts."

"But what happened?" my mother asked, sitting up, and glancing at Nompumelelo, who was not in the least concerned, just standing there, rubbing her eyes and yawning.

"We were busy preparing tea and scones at the minister's house just after midnight, when one of the doorkeepers from the concert hall came up to me and told me to follow him because my younger sister needed me."

"Then?" asked my father, looking from Nompumelelo to Nombulelo and back.

"I went with him, and there she was," Nombulelo said, still sounding cross. "Standing half dressed in the hall and everybody looking at her! At first I didn't understand what was going on, until one of the choir members explained that Nompumelelo had fallen asleep on the bench and had slept right through all the activities around her. Until she suddenly got up and started to undress!"

Members of the Chapel Street Methodist Church Women's *Manyano*, 1959, dressed in their uniforms to have their picture taken with Rev. Pitso. Some of the women sang in the church choir. Some years before, my sister Nombulelo used to stay up with Rev. Zwane's daughter, Joy, to serve tea and scones when the choir performed at the regular all-night concerts.

My mother smiled. "I'm sure she must have been in a daze and thought that she was home."

"Home! How could she ever think that, with so many people around her? Was I embarrassed!"

"Come on, Nombulelo, she must have been doing it in her sleep," my father tried to console his eldest daughter.

"How did you get back this time of the night?" my mother suddenly asked.

"Joy's brother and his friends walked us home." Nombulelo got angry again. "Mama, I'll never again take Nompumelelo along to a night concert. She's too young. She really spoilt my evening!"

"Don't worry, we won't allow her to go again," my father promised.

"Let her get some sleep, we'll talk about this in the morning," Mama suggested.

OTHER ENTERTAINMENT

Musical groups from Johannesburg also came to Cape Town to stage shows like *King Kong*, and so on. In most cases they were accommodated at the Tafelberg Hotel in Constitution Street. It was easy for us to meet famous stars like Dorothy Masuka, Patience Africa and Dolly Rathebe, to name but a few, because we used to visit them at the hotel and watch them rehearse.

When I was in Std 3, Dorothy Masuka even visited our school in Langa. She came one Friday afternoon and sang to us in our school hall. When she started singing her smashing hit "Notsokolo", we all jumped up and down in our seats. The principal did not like that, but he pretended not to see because everybody liked the music.

The Boswell Circus also regularly visited Cape Town. They pitched their tents on the Foreshore and the residents were fond of walking down there from District Six to look at the caged animals.

One day Mzwandile's brother and a young man named Dodo decided to go down to the Foreshore. It was a Sunday afternoon. When they came back, Mzwandile's brother calmly told my father that he had nearly been attacked by a bear.

"A bear?" asked my father, very surprised.

"Yes, at the circus."

"*Inene,* Hambani? Is it true? I can't believe it!" my father said.

"Well, there were a couple of bears locked in cages. And there was a sign DO NOT COME TOO CLOSE on the side of the cage. But I didn't see it. I was looking the other way and moved back so close to the cage that when the bear put his paw through the iron bars, it touched my jacket. It hooked his claws into the fabric and started to pull."

"*Awu!*" we children exclaimed.

"At first, I thought that it was Dodo, because I was still not looking behind me. But the screaming of some of the circus staff brought me back to reality.

"'Look out! Look out!' they yelled. When I turned around, there was this big animal, right behind me, growling and pulling at the pocket of my jacket. *Thiza!* Did I get a fright! The next moment, the man in charge of the bears came running with an iron rod in his hands. He waved it in the air and the bear let go of my pocket and moved back."

My father shook his head in disbelief.

"The pocket of the jacket was ripped off, but the bear trainer saved my life."

"*Nkosi yami!*" exclaimed my father. "My word! The last time I heard of bears attacking people was in a story from the Bible – *II Kings*, Chapter 2, verse 24."

Everyone started laughing.

"I hope you haven't done anything wrong, Hambani. When last have you sent money to your wife?" my father asked Mzwandile's brother with a broad smile.

THE FIRST WHITE WEDDING

The first white wedding in the Black community of District Six was celebrated in 1954.

It was a Saturday morning, when a shrieking voice drew the attention of the residents of Cross Street.

"*Halala! Nguwo nguwo ngumtshato! Halala!*" – It's a wedding day – we heard.

MaNyawuza, Zibi's wife, was coming out of No. 22's front door, followed by a group of women who were shrieking and moving around excitedly.

"*Yavela inkosazana! Vulani amabala!*" – Give way, the princess is coming! – they shouted, clearing the way for the bride.

Hombakazi, the bride, two flower girls and the bridesmaids were emerging from No. 22 and led to the sparkling Studebaker cars that were waiting in front of the house to take them to church in Langa.

Hombakazi was getting married to Douglas Bunyula, also a resident of District Six. He lived about twelve yards from Cross Street over in William Street and was a regular visitor of the Njobe family's. So he and Hombakazi often saw each other at Cross Street, but since both attended the Anglican church in Langa, the wedding ceremony was to be held in Langa.

Outside in the street a group of young Black men and women were singing and clapping their hands. They were singing wedding songs, like *"Vela langa kutshata inkosazana"* – Shine, sun, shine, the princess is getting married.

The bridesmaids, in their orange dresses with long skirts, white gloves and white shoes, waited near the cars while the bride was being helped into the back seat of the grandest car. She was in a beautiful white dress with a long satin skirt and a bodice covered with lace. Her gloves were fancier than the bridemaids' gloves and her face was covered by a white veil. She looked exceptionally beautiful.

The two flower girls could not wait to get on to the front seat of the car. In their orange dresses with short skirts and matching orange bows on their heads, they helped each other into the bridal car. After the bridesmaids had got inside the second, black Studebaker, a loud shriek from the women drowned the sound of the running engines.

"Halala! Halala! Nguwo, nguwo-o-o!" – This is it!

From all directions Coloured people were attracted by the music, for it was clear that this wedding was quite different from the usual Muslim weddings seen in District Six, with the bride and bridesmaids glittering in horse-drawn chariots. This wedding had less glitter but a lot more movement and music. The blending of deep and high-pitched voices sent every bystander moving to the tune.

As soon as the wedding party were settled in the cars, the drivers started hooting, slowly steering the cars down Richmond into Stuckeris Street, and on their way to Langa.

The hooting caused more excitement, with the women shrieking and moving sideways and around, waving their jerseys and handkerchiefs.

"Halala! Halala!"

Young children ran after the cars, trying to steal a last glimpse of the bride, while the older people remained standing in the street, talking about how lovely she looked.

"Where are they going?" asked a Coloured resident.

"To church in Langa, but they're coming back in the afternoon."

"Good! I don't want to miss them when they do. You people sing and dance so well."

The highlight was the afternoon. A large number of people who had attended the church ceremony returned to welcome the bridal couple. The bride and groom walked up and down Cross Street, stepping to the rhythm of songs and the clapping of hands.

Then stick-fighting started. Some of the young men formed a circle, with one man in the centre. He pointed at someone in the circle, challenging him to a fight.

"Mthathe mfana!" the others encouraged the one who had been challenged – Take him, man!

The challenged man would thereupon step into the centre and display his stick-fighting skills as never before.

The Coloured residents did not understand that it was not real fighting, but just a game. *"Hierdie mense het wragtag harde koppe,"* a Coloured guy observed while watching the goings-on. "With those knocks on my head I would bleed to death."

The blows were not as hard as he imagined. The skill was in the graceful movement, which allowed the player to catch his opponent unawares. It was almost like a game of tennis.

While the old men were praising the best stick-fighter, the women were spreading rugs on the ground in front of the bride and groom, shrieking and dancing.

A reception followed at the Clyde Street hall that evening. The bride and groom had changed into evening wear, she into a plain evening gown, he into a different colour suit. After opening the floor with the first dance of the evening, the couple sat down at a table with the bridesmaids to enjoy some snacks.

The traditional singing of earlier now made way for a hired band who played soft music. One of District Six's *maskanda*s played the piano, some Coloured guys blew saxophones, and a tall African man was the drummer. People were waltzing around the hall.

As was the custom, some of the guests presented gifts and donated money at a table on the side of the hall, not far from the exit. Everybody looked beautiful under the electric light, especially the young ladies gliding around in their long evening dresses of satin or velvet.

Just then, somebody screamed, *"Imali! Imali!"* – The money!

Everybody came to a standstill, except for a young man named Mzwebedu. He was running like blazes towards the door with the bags of money in his hands.

"Mbambeni! Catch him! Catch him!" shouted one of the men who was sitting at the table. But it was too late. The young chap was already flying down the flight of stairs, three and four at a time, out into the street.

Mzwebedu, we were told, had recently arrived in District Six from Johannesburg. The local residents did not like him because he used of lot of slang. Instead of asking, "Where do you live?" he would say, *"Waa phola jy?"* Because "tsotsi taal" was unacceptable, Mzwebedu was not only seen as a tsotsi but also as a bad influence on the youth of the neighbourhood.

After the incident, everybody was on the lookout for Mzwebedu, but the matter was not reported to the police because Mzwebedu was the groom's homeboy. After a week of searching for him, it was assumed that he had left District Six. This was later confirmed by one of his relatives in Johannesburg, who knew of the robbery. In a letter to one of the residents this man wrote that he had recently seen Mzwebedu loitering on the streets of the City of Gold.

But Mzwebedu did not disrupt the reception for long. Solomon Mpazi, as head of the Cross Street disciplinary committee, assured the guests that everything was under control.

"Baphi abatshati?" – Where are the newly weds? – he enquired. And urging the band to play on, he said, "Lead us to the next dance!"

The groom did not waste time. He swung his bride onto the floor, waltzing to the sweet tune of "Good night, Irene, good night, Irene, I'll see you in my dreams ..."

THE *AMAMFENGU* CELEBRATION

On the 14th of May each year a Fingo – *amaMfengu* – celebration was staged at Langa. On this day all the Fingo residents of District Six used to attire themselves in their traditional dress and go to the Langa Civic Hall where a feast had been organised by the *amaMfengu* who lived in the township.

A number of cattle and sheep were slaughtered and the meat was prepared, together with samp and some vegetables, in big, three-legged pots on fires outside the hall. African beer was also prepared, well in advance.

But there was a more official part to the celebration. During a ceremony one of the elders would relate the history of the *amaMfengu*, and their historic oath, made in 1835, would be repeated three times. The *imbongi* – praise-singer – would then sing praise songs in memory of the chiefs who died so many years ago, as well as the praises of some other more recent heroes. This would be followed by various groups displaying Fingo dances and performing traditional songs. A choir from one of the local schools would round off this part of the celebration with the classic song "Fourteenth of May".

Our Coloured neighbours used to enjoy watching us dress up in our beautiful, brightly coloured outfits, and would ask permission to take photographs.

We had a lot of explanation to do about the meaning of this day, even to some of the other African people, because not all Black residents of Cross Street were involved with or belonged to the *amaMfengu* ethnic group.

The Fingos were originally from the north of the country, from Zulu-

Mamiya Makhabane with Mrs Mamtanda (right) in traditional Fingo attire. Mrs Mamtanda used to be a "sleep in" domestic, so the photograph, taken at Maxim's Studio, probably records the way the two friends were dressed for an *amaMfengu* celebration in Langa one 14th of July.

land. But during the great wars of King Shaka, they gradually moved down the east coast and eventually settled in Transkei. In fact, the name "Mfengu" originated from the verb "ukumfenguza" – to flee, moving from place to place, looking for peace.

After the Fingos had made Transkei their home, some English soldiers arrived, who requested a meeting with the three Fingo chiefs, Mhlambiso, Njokweni and Mabandla. At that meeting, the chiefs indicated that it had always been their wish to move further south. So the Reverend Ayliff of the Methodist Church initiated the removal of the Fingo people from the area. He had identified land for them between two rivers, the Fish River and the Keiskamma.

All this happened in 1835.

Ayliff's aim was to convert the Fingos to Christianity and make them members of the Methodist Church. After their arrival in Ciskei, the area to the south of Transkei, the Fingos were assembled at Peddie under a tree known as *umqwashu*. Here they had to take the following oath to the missionary –

To worship the living God.
To educate their children.
To always abide by the laws of the government in place.

The undertaking was repeated three times. This event meant a lot to the *amaMfengu* and from then on it was always celebrated on the 14th of May each year.

The *amaMfengu* were the first Africans to trade with the Whites. They became skilled in agriculture, especially those living around Fort Beaufort. Their closeness to and co-operation with Whites, as well as their non-participation in the national suicide of the *amaXhosa* in 1857, was seen by other ethnic groups as treachery.

Much later, during the time that Chief Lennox Sebe and his governing Ikhonkco party ruled in Ciskei, from about 1974 to the late 1980s, descendants of this group formed the majority of Chief Justice Mabandla's opposition party Imbokodo. So once again the Fingos were unpopular with the other Africans living in the Eastern Cape, and it was during this time that the ruling party put a stop to the Fingo celebration, and in its place promoted the *Intaba kaNdoda* celebration.

A shrine was built at the top of Intaba kaNdoda, and during the Easter weekend the Ciskeian ruling party organised a celebration on top of the mountain, which was mostly attended by government supporters and functionaries. The *Intaba kaNdoda* celebration promoted Xhosa rather than Fingo ethnicity.

Of course the African freedom fighters and political activists were not at all in favour of promoting ethnicity, which they believed was at the heart of both the *amaMfengu* celebration and the *Intaba kaNdoda* celebration. They strongly discouraged any such events, as this was seen as the White's tool of dividing the African community.

Before these tensions came out in the open, however, we happily put on our Fingo outfits and celebrated the 14th of May.

The Sunday afternoon spends at the halls in Clyde, Ayre and Primrose Street were very popular with the Black residents of District Six. The shows, which lasted from about two o'clock in the afternoon until ten o'clock at night, were arranged into two sessions. The first half was for vocal music by various groups, like our own Mills Brothers, and groups from Langa. It was expected of the audience to keep still and listen. During the second half of the programme, dance and jive music was played by bands like the Merry Macs from Langa, and sometimes, bands from the Muslim community.

Drinks were sold and because some African men were dating Coloured women, some mixed couples also attended.

It was impressive indeed to see the young ladies in their best dresses being escorted by their male friends to these functions. Formal dress had to be worn and everybody adhered to this stipulation. People treated each other with courtesy and everybody was there to enjoy the show after a hard week's work. The admission fee was very reasonable, and so the shows got a lot of support.

I was sixteen when my father allowed me to go to my first afternoon spend. I was very excited though I knew I would only be able to enjoy the first part, during which vocal music was rendered, and the first hour of the more exciting dance and jive music session, because before Nompumelelo and I left my father had warned, "Nompumelelo, you must be back by half past seven."

"Ewe, Tata. We won't be late," Nompumelelo promised.

I was dressed in navy blue and white. I had on a straight white skirt with a pleat at the back, a navy blue and white striped blouse, and navy-and-white "baby heel" shoes to match – plus stockings with a seam at the back. I looked much older than a sixteen-year-old schoolgirl!

"It's hot today, so I'm sure the show is going to be full," remarked Nompumelelo, as we walked down Hanover Street.

When we approached the hall at Ayre Street, a group of people were waiting at the entrance.

"You see? I told you," Nompumelelo said. "Let's rush for the front seats, I want you to see everything, Nomvuyo."

We got in quickly. A double quartet from Langa were already performing on the stage. Some of my school mates were sitting in front and we went to join them. I knew most of the songs and I really enjoyed the music.

Came the time for dance and jive, the master of ceremonies requested the audience to leave their seats so that the chairs could be placed on one side of the hall to allow space for dancing. I could not yet dance, so I stood next to the wall with some of my school mates and watched. When the band played "Martial Law", a big hit right then, we young ones took over the stage, swinging, twisting, turning, throwing, and stamping our feet. It was wonderful!

Just then, Nompumelelo came up to me. "Nomvuyo, time's up. We must go," she said.

"Oh no! The fun's just starting," I pleaded.

Masihambe, man. Let's go, you know Tata. If we get back late, this will be your first and last time to an afternoon spend."

Knowing my father the way I did, I quickly turned around, waved to my friends and left.

After a show a string of couples would always be seen walking towards the bus stops in Hanover Street. From there they would catch different buses to the various surburbs where the ladies were employed as "live-in" domestic servants.

Two days after the afternoon spend, I was with Nompumelelo at home when she started laughing as if she had just remembered something.

"Hey, Nomvuyo, strange things are really happening in Sea Point," she said and burst out laughing again.

"Please share the joke," I said, rather interested in what was coming.

"Do you know Bhut'Sizwe from Stuckeris Street? He was at the show the other day."

"Yes, I saw him jiving with a tall, beautiful woman."

"That's right. That lady is his girlfriend. After the show, I understand, they went together to Sea Point." Nompumelelo stopped and started laughing again.

"Come on, what's the joke?" I asked, becoming impatient.

"When they got off the bus at Sea Point, apparently a police van had been following them. But it went past and so they thought that they'd escaped the law …"

"These men never give up!" I interrupted her. "How many cases of arrests for trespassing have been reported, but they still insist on going to the White surburbs!"

"Do you think that the arrests will stop them? *Andiqondi* – I don't think so. What they do is pay an admission of guilt and then they're set free again," Nompumelelo explained.

"But what happened to Bhut'Sizwe?" I remembered.

"They safely got to his girlfriend's workplace at a flat in one of the back streets. About fifteen minutes later, they heard a loud knock at the door of the servants' quarters."

"'It's the Police! Open up!'

"Bhut'Sizwe jumped out of bed. His girlfriend quickly helped him into her nightie and doek and he got back into bed. The girlfriend opened the door. There stood two White policemen.

"'Pass, mama!' said one. The lady went for her bag.

"'What are you waiting for, where's your pass?' the policeman asked Bhut'Sizwe who was at this stage looking like Sisi Sizwe."

We both burst out laughing and I said, "I'm sure he passed well as Sisi Sizwe. At least he has a shaven face."

"What about the pass? That would clearly have indicated that he was a man!" Nompumelelo said, smiling.

"I hope he wasn't stupid enough to show it," I said.

"Oh no! It would have given the game away, so he decided to say that he did not have it with him. He was clever enough to talk like a woman.

"'You're under arrest!' said the policeman, 'Get up and get dressed!'"

Apparently when Sisi Sizwe got out of bed, his legs showed, and so the policeman said, *"Nee, man! Daar's iets verkeerd hierso! Kyk, ou maat,"* he referred to his friend. *"Dis glad nie 'n vroumens hierdie nie!"* – This is not a woman! And he grabbed the doek from Bhut'Sizwe's head.

"You bastard! Of course you're a man!"

"Sorry, my baas," pleaded Bhut'Sizwe. His lady friend quickly took his clothes from the wardrobe. He was not even given a chance to dress fully before he was taken out of the room and thrown into the van.

Later we heard that he was charged with trespassing, but he happily paid the fine because he and his girlfriend had almost outwitted the officers.

9

THE BUSY BEE RUGBY CLUB

In the mid-1930s, three men, one from District Six (Mr Njobe) and two business men from Langa (Mr Gcilishe and Mr Charlton Nabe) formed a rugby club known as the Busy Bee. The two Langa shop owners donated the players' first kits – jerseys, shorts, socks, and rugby boots – and Mr Njobe was elected manager of the team. The majority of players were recruited from Ciskei and a few others came from elsewhere in the Eastern Cape.

The team was registered with the Langa Rugby Football Union and played matches at Langa against Langa teams like Mother City, Bantu and Thembu.

The green-and-white Busy Bee kit was identical to that of a White rugby team from False Bay, so later the players from False Bay used to give unwanted kit to the growing Busy Bee team. This no doubt must have helped Mr Gcilishe and Mr Charlton Nabe.

Later, Ivan Fuzani, who came from Port Elizabeth, joined the team. He was the inspiration of Black rugby in the Western Cape, a good player who was nominated captain of the Busy Bee a year after he joined. He stayed in Roger Street and shortly after he became captain, he recruited Mr Luke from Bryant Street, BoKaap, for the team. This was a good move, because from 1939 to 1941 the Busy Bee were winners of the League Cup. Luke had played for a Coloured team called the Stars before that.

My father and Mr Fuzani were good friends because they both originally came from Fort Beaufort, where they grew up in the same neighbourhood and attended the same school. Before he came to live in Cape Town, Mr Fuzani first went to work on the mines in Johannesburg. My father did not do that. He moved straight here.

Tata used to tell us what a good sportsman Ivan Fuzani was. Whenever he did, he always talked about the day of the final League match in 1941, when the Busy Bee won the Cup. He himself could not go to the match that Saturday afternoon because he had to work overtime.

"Everybody at Cross Street was excited on that day and quite a number of the male residents went to watch the match at Langa," my father said. It was around six-thirty in the afternoon when I heard a group of people singing the Busy Bee song *'Yingwe emabalabala le Busy Bee'* – It's a tiger with stripes, this Busy Bee.

"I quickly ran to the window and saw Fuzani holding the cup. He held it up high, and when he saw me he shouted, 'We've m-made it, Jimmy!' using my name from our cricket team."

"It sounds exciting, Tata," Layton always remarked at this point and immediately enquired, "And then?"

"The other players," my father continued, "were holding up their rugby jerseys with the stripes, and singing and marching up and down Cross Street in front of the building. Some of the male residents, who like myself couldn't go to the match, joined in the singing and marching, and the women started clapping their hands and putting some money into the trophy.

"'Where is the captain?' asked Mr Morris, one of the Coloured neighbours. 'Carry him on your shoulders with the trophy! We want to see him!' he shouted.

"Fuzani was swooped off his feet, high up, still holding the trophy, and the Coloured neighbours started a silver collection."

"Tat'uFuzani must have been a happy man," said Layton with envy.

"Oh yes, my son, he was all smiles that day."

My father would pause and then continue, "That evening we put some money together and bought bottles of beer and gathered in the kitchen at No. 22, where we even forgot about the police raids and talked about how the match was won, until late at night."

"*Bantwana bam*," my mother once said, joining in the conversation, "my children, they were so excited and made so much noise that Mrs Njobe and I decided to sit and chat over a cup of tea with my raisin loaf because we couldn't sleep."

"Even the police wouldn't stop us on that day," my father boasted, a big smile on his face.

After winning the League Cup in 1941, the players put money together for a big celebration at the Clyde Street hall. This would be a sign of giving thanks to their ancestors for seeing them through the League competition.

Before the celebration, a series of meetings were held with the officials of the team as well as the players and fans at the Strong Yard in Roger Street where Fuzani lived. The amount needed for the celebration was worked out and it was discussed how the money would be raised – that is, through donations from officials, players, fans and other teams belonging to the Union. The money from the other teams was, of

The proud Busy Bee rugby team who won the Langa Rugby Football League cup three years in succession, from 1939 to 1941. Middle row, 3rd from left is Ivan Fuzani, the captain; 2nd from left is Michael Tsika who made the moving speech at Fuzani's funeral. Mr Luke, 2nd from the left, 3rd row, is the only former Busy Bee player still alive.

The officials of the Busy Bee Rugby Club, 1939. Mr Charlton Nabe (front row, 2nd from left) and Mr Gcilishe (2nd from right), two Langa businessmen, bought the team's first kits. Mr Njobe (on right) was the manager. Behind him stands Douglas Bunyula, the groom at the first Black "white wedding" in District Six.

course, *umgalelo*, which meant it would be repaid when those teams had their celebrations.

After working out their income and expenditure, the organisers listed the names of guests and worked out a short programme for the day.

"We'll leave the buying and delivery of the ox to you, since you both have vans," said Njobe, the manager, to the two business men Gcilishe and Nabe.

"Oh, leave it to us, we've already spoken to one of the butchers from Langa. He'll go with us to a farm in Stellenbosch; all we need from you is the money, as well as the names of four young men who'll accompany us to the farm and assist us with the loading and delivery," replied Nabe.

"The f-f-four young men w-w-will be Gosa, Phakamisa, Zolisa and S-S-Staarman," Fuzani said, pointing to the four.

"*Hayi ho!* Oh no!" protested Zolisa. "Why me, Bhut'Fuz, when there is Themba Memani?"

"*Suk'apha,* Zolisa! – Get away from here! The captain is right, you should go. Don't you know that I'm older than you?" Themba teased.

A whole argument about age started among the group, some joking about the choice of helpers until it was finally decided that Themba would go instead of Zolisa.

On the day of the slaughtering, which was a Saturday, the day before the celebration, all the Busy Bee players and officials again gathered at Strong Yard. They were casually dressed, some in overalls, in preparation for the big job that lay ahead. One of the players had brought along a spear. The ox was delivered early that morning.

After the beast's legs and horns were tied, the men made it lie down on its side. Fuzani advanced with the spear and swiftly pierced it on one side. The animal bellowed. All the men shouted with excitement.

"*Izinyanya zivumile, itheko maliqhube!*" – The ancestors agree that the show must go on! – one of the elders shouted.

"Come on, young men, carry on with the slaughtering. Fuzani has done his job," instructed Njobe.

Everybody was congratulating Fuzani on his good work.

"*Uyindoda,* Fuzani!" – You're a man! The two business men patted him on his shoulder. According to African culture, an occasion does not have the blessings of the ancestors if the ox does not bellow at the piercing.

"Bring the dishes!" shouted Themba.

Mrs Fuzani brought along African beer and the men started drinking.

"*Bumnandi obu tywala!* – This beer is very tasty. Who taught you to make beer, Mrs Fuzani?"

"Stop asking questions, Gatyeni, drink the beer or pass it on, we're thirsty!" shouted one man, sitting in a corner.

"*Hamba bhekile!*" – Pass it on! – another shouted.

On the Sunday morning, a number of women, mostly the wives of players and officials, went to Roger Street to cook the meat, samp, potatoes and carrots. Some of the young men assisted with the fire and the lifting of the big, three-legged pots.

When the food was cooked, the pots and barrels of African beer were loaded on to the two vans and taken to the Clyde Street hall.

Quite a number of people had already gathered here, the Langa Rugby Football Union officials, players from other Langa teams, a few women, children. The Busy Bee players soon arrived in their green blazers, white shirts, grey trousers, and green-and-white striped ties.

"Ladies and gentlemen, may I have your attention," Njobe started. When everybody was quiet, the ceremony was opened with a short prayer by Charlton Nabe.

The team members were then asked to go and stand on the stage with the trophy.

The one and only speech was made by Mr Gcilishe.

"Officials of the Langa Rugby Football Union, the Busy Bees' manager, Mr Njobe, the captain of the Busy Bees, Mr Fuzani, and his team, the teams from Langa, residents of District Six and children," he said, looking at everyone in turn. "A word of welcome to you all. We're gathered here today to congratulate our team, the Busy Bee Rugby Club, on their third consecutive success in winning the League Cup.

"Africans, I know, believe *okwesithathu ngumnqakathi* – that the third time around is always contrary to expectations – but today, our team has proved that saying wrong ..."

The hall roared with laughter, and there was loud applause.

The speaker paused for a while, a broad smile on his face. After the noise had died down, he continued, "Oom Fuz and your team, you're great and you've made us proud. Thank you for bringing the trophy back. Today, ladies and gentlemen, is not a day for speeches. That was done by the Langa Union officials at Langa stadium on the day of the final. I'm only standing here today to tell you the reason we have slaughtered an ox because I know that Africans don't usually enjoy slaughtered meat without having a reason for the occasion. With these few words, I invite you to feel at home and join us in our excitement."

In his excitement about his team winning the League, Ivan Fuzani bought a trophy and donated it to the Langa Rugby Football Union. It was known as the Fuzani Cup. The Busy Bee players developed a special emotional attachment to this cup, and vowed they would never allow another team to win the trophy. There was quite a special feel to that team! Former players would encourage their sons to play for the

Busy Bee Club, too. So in the end, generation after generation of players came from the same families – the Gcilishes, Ncapais, Zixeshas, and so on.

THE LADIES' SECTION

Amazing things happened in the mid-1950s. The Busy Bee Rugby Club started a ladies' section! This was actually not so strange: it was common practice with the Langa Rugby Football Union teams. It is more amazing to think about it now, because almost forty years ago, Black women were being involved in rugby, a sport seen today as predominantly male, and White.

So what is the difference between this and women's empowerment in sport? The difference is that in those days, the women did not play rugby. They joined to support the teams, and organise their entertainment, as well as to cater and fund-raise. My sister Nompumelelo was the secretary of the Busy Bees' ladies' section.

By this time Nompumelelo had already left school. After completing Std 8 (what is now Grade 10), she started working as a domestic servant for a White family in Rondebosch, about fifteen kilometres from District Six. She had made friends with Virginia, another domestic servant in the area. One day Virginia said, "Nompumelelo, what do you do on Sunday afternoons when you're off?"

"Why?" Nompumelelo asked, surprised at the question.

"Please answer me," Virginia insisted.

"Okay, I usually stay at home with my family and go to church in the evenings."

"Would you like to join our ladies' section at the Busy Bee Club? We need young people like you who have stayed at school longer than we did," Virginia said.

"What does this ladies' section do?"

"It's fun, you'll see. We watch matches at Langa when the Busy Bee rugby team play, and cheer them."

"Is that all?"

"No, sometimes we hold meetings to discuss other activities."

"Such as?"

"You know … entertainment, fund-raising for the club, and so."

"When do you do all this?"

"Only on Sunday afternoons when everybody is free. All the members are, just like us, domestic servants."

"Sounds interesting, but I'll have to talk to my parents about it."

"Please do. We need someone who can be our secretary," Virginia pleaded.

"Not so fast, I'm not sure if my father will buy it."

My parents had no problem with the proposition. My father, in fact, encouraged Nompumelelo to join because he knew the other members to be responsible adults, and he was sure that she would be in good hands. My brother Layton, at this stage, was also showing a lot of interest in rugby. He played it at school and liked to go to Langa on Sunday afternoons to watch the matches.

A year after Nompumelelo joined the club, she was elected secretary, a job she enjoyed very much. She wrote the minutes of the meetings, dealt with correspondence (in most cases invitations from other clubs), and also wrote notices of meetings. Unless there was an urgent matter to be discussed, these meetings were held once a month, in the kitchen at No. 22 Cross Street.

In the late 1950s, the Busy Bee Club were so prominent that they hosted teams from the Eastern Cape and Border over Easter weekends. The ladies' section prepared meals for the visiting teams and arranged beauty pageants for entertainment and to raise funds.

In fact, rugby was so established among Black people then that tournaments were held at provincial level, with Western Province, Midlands, Border and Eastern Province playing each other.

It worked this way: a provincial team was picked from the teams registered with the Langa Rugby Football Union. At the time, the Busy Bee Club boasted a very high standard, and provincial players like "Staarman" Mkiva played for them, with the result that a strong love of rugby developed amongst the Black residents of District Six. Hundreds of rugby fans would flock to Langa stadium to watch the tournament, and support their side. The excitement reached fever pitch during tough matches at the time of the popular Eastern Province fly-half, Eric Majola, Western Province wing Bobby Siboto, nicknamed "Bob Scott", and the Border centre, Talase Myute.

After the provincial tournament, a Springbok team would be picked to play against the Coloured Springbok team at Green Point stadium.

I still remember that my uncle, Philemon Ngcelwane, who was an official of the Border Rugby Football Union, would come all the way from King William's Town to the tournament with his team.

All the teams from the Eastern Cape came in hired buses and were accommodated at schools, because the tournament used to take place during the June school vacation. Different schools were used to accomodate different teams, so that each provincial team could have their privacy. The final lists of teams were usually kept a secret and the training

WESTERN PROVINCE BANTU RUGBY TEAM
WINNERS OF ZONK TROPHY   CAPE TOWN, 1958

Some members of the Busy Bee played for the Western Province African rugby team. 2nd row from back, on left: Bobby Siboto; 4th from left: Phakie Gcilishe, and on right: "Staarman" Mkiva. "Kuku" Kuse, 3rd from left at the back, lived in Wicht Street in District Six.

Bobby "Bob Scott" Siboto was the fastest Black Western Province wing. Here he is chasing the ball with typical speed.

mornings to avoid the public. All this secrecy, I believe, added to the excitement.

"Does your team have a good chance this time, Philemon?" my father asked his brother one year.

"I hope so, Bhuti. We worked very hard this year, though it's difficult to tell at this stage, because the teams have not been announced yet. All I know is that Eric Majola from Eastern Province is still there and we don't have a fly-half to match him."

"Don't worry, Mbele, he can't do anything on his own. Rugby is team work," my father said, reassuring him.

"That's true, Bhuti," Uncle Philemon agreed.

"Which teams are playing the first match?"

"Well, it's supposed to be the hosting team and the winner of the last tournament … . Oh yes, it's Western Province against Eastern Province."

"Wow! That match will surely attract a big crowd," my father said excitedly.

"Oh yes! Anyway, that'll give us a chance to judge their style and strategise accordingly."

"Don't be so sure, there's good rugby in the Eastern Province."

"You're right, Bhuti. Coaches will probably make slight changes in their teams for each match. Anyway, we've decided to reserve Myute for the tougher matches."

On the first day of the tournament, Layton got up early and made himself a lunch-box for the day.

"I want to get a good seat on the stand," he explained when my mother asked him why he was up so early. When he came back that evening, he was full of excitement.

"Mama, it's a good thing I left early this morning. When I got to the stadium, the queues were very long. We had to wait for about half an hour before we could pay and get inside the stadium. It was so cold we bought some soup from a lady near the stand."

"Did you see your uncle at the stadium?"

"Yes, Mama, he bought me some peanuts and oranges."

"Did his team win?" asked my mother.

"Hayi khona, Mama, it was Western Province and Eastern Province playing today. Border, Uncle's team, will play the day after tomorrow," explained Layton, shaking his head.

"Don't bother to explain, *mntwan'am* – my child. I don't understand these things, anyway. You can talk to your father about it."

"How did it go, Layton?" my father asked when he got back later that evening.

"Hee, Tata, I don't know where to start."

"Start from the beginning," my father said, pulling up his chair.

"Tata! It was a *shushu,* a really hot game. Can you believe that the score was six all at half time?"

"Hayi suka! Tell me about Majola."

"The Western Province players were watching him like hawks, but Tata, that guy is very good. He scored the try that put Eastern Province ahead in the second half."

"I told Philemon about Eastern Province. By the way, did you see him at the stadium?"

"Ewe, Tata. We were together throughout. I heard him cry out *'Nank'uMajola!'* – Here's Majola! – when the fly-half made a good move, and *'Hayi khona!'* when the Western Province forwards tackled him. He sure was excited and really enjoyed the game."

"What was the final score?"

"Six-nine, in favour of Eastern Province."

"That was close!" my father exclaimed.

"Ewe. Tata, and Western Province were playing a pass ball. From the scrum-half to the fly-half, by-passing the inside centre to the outside

centre, then to the outside wing! 'Bob Scott! Bobby!' shouted the crowd but the Eastern Province lock was already waiting and pushed him out. The crowd applauded, very excited about the outstanding move and everybody agreed that even if Western Province lost the match, they had really played a good game."

"How does Philemon feel about his team?"

"I'm sure he's worried. I heard him say the standard was very high and that it would take a very strong team to beat Eastern Province."

My father smiled in reply.

THE TRY AGAIN CRICKET CLUB

My father got his nickname "Jimmy" in the Try Again Cricket Club for which he played, because two other club members were also named James. It was Ivan Fuzani who had the idea to call my father "Jimmy".

Apart from rugby, the Black residents of District Six also played cricket. What is interesting is that Mr Njobe, who managed the rugby club, was a manager in cricket as well.

Apart from the people who acted as officials for rugby and doubled up doing the same for cricket, some new people became involved – like Mr Mshumpela, the father of the former principal of St Cyprian's School in Langa, Alex "Nozulu" Mshumpela, who lived in William Street. Alex, in fact, was the score-keeper of the team.

Like the manager and some of the officials, players from the Busy Bee rugby team were also involved in the the Try Again Cricket Club. Fuzani, for instance, was the best bowler of the team. Other players were Michael Tsika, Gibson "the Xhwele" Gcilishe, who was a traditional healer, and Zixesha, who was known as Zi "Time".

My mother, a member of the ladies' section of the Try Again Cricket Club, was a staunch supporter of the team and sometimes went to watch matches at Langa.

Later, when she told them about the good times that she and my father had those days, it had always sounded like a joke to her grandsons Andile, Rooi, Selby and Babini. She would say, "Your grandfather was a very good batsman. He would hit a series of sixes and not even show any excitement about it. The crowd would scream, 'Jimmy, *babonise!* – Show them!' but he would pretend not to hear and just watch the bowler."

Her grandchildren smiled but did not take her seriously until they watched a cricket match on television with her one day. Suddenly she proved her knowledge of cricket by shouting, "He's out!" when the ball appeared to hit the leg pads of the batsman. When the umpire indicated

Cricket was never quite as popular as rugby, but the Try Again Cricket Club shared some players and officials with the Busy Bee Rugby Club – like Mr Njobe (back, left) the manager, and Ivan Fuzani (front, left). My father, "Jimmy" Ngcelwane, is standing to the right of Gibson "the Xhwele" Gcilishe (3rd from right, back).

Six years later, in 1941, Mr Njobe (back, left) is still manager of the Try Again Cricket Club. My father, too, (back, 3rd from right) was also still in the team, and so were Michael Tsika (to his right) and Ivan Fuzani (front, right).

that the player was indeed out, the boys looked at their grandmother with new respect.

"Old girl, I'm beginning to believe you now. You know cricket better than any of us here!" Rooi said, calling her by our favourite name for my mother. All of us took this term of endearment from a White lady who used to phone to find out if my mother was still keeping well. My mother worked for her for twelve years before she retired. Mrs Sargosky would always begin the conversation with, "How's the old girl?"

"My grandchild, I was not born yesterday, you know?" my mother replied, smiling.

In Hanover Street, next to the public wash-house, there used to be a swimming pool and baths for Black men only. It still puzzles me that a recreational structure of this nature was reserved for Blacks only, in an area which was predominantly Coloured. In any event, the Black men came in big numbers to the baths, especially on Sunday mornings. This is where they discussed their rugby team's performance and what changes needed to be made to the team or its playing strategy.

Staying away from the baths for one week meant that you fell behind in your knowledge of the latest rugby developments. Cricket was not as popular as rugby, so it was hardly ever mentioned. Besides rugby, politics were discussed in a big way at the baths.

SAD NEWS ABOUT A GREAT HERO

In the mid-1950s Ivan Fuzani, the best African sportsman District Six ever saw, fell ill. He took a long sick leave, but still his health deteriorated. He became weaker by the day.

I heard my father say to my mother after coming back from visiting his friend in Roger Street one Saturday afternoon, "I've been to Fuzani this afternoon, and you know, he doesn't look good. He tried to bluff me by cracking jokes but I noticed that he's become weaker."

"That's very sad," was my mother's comment.

It was a Saturday morning, just after ten o'clock, a few weeks later, and my parents were both at home. My mother was busy dictating a list of items I had to get from the shop, when there was a soft knock at the door. My mother was standing at the table, kneading dough to bake the raisin loaf that evening, which was her usual Saturday routine. My father was sitting in his armchair reading the morning's paper.

It was Bhut'Thole from Roger Street. He had come to tell us that Fuzani had died that morning. Though my father had feared that all was not well with his friend, nothing had prepared him for this blow.

"Awu, uFuzani? Yini uFuzani madoda!" my father exclaimed. My mother, blue from shock, threw herself into a chair. I raised my eyebrows but did not move or say anything.

"I remember what he said last time I visited him, the day before yesterday," my father softly said. Stammering the way he always did, he said, 'Jimmy, my road is coming to an end. I don't think I'll be able to go back to work again.'"

At that moment we heard loud footsteps coming up the stairs. It was Solomon Mpazi, who had also just heard the sad news. The two men decided to go to Roger Street, to give support to Fuzani's widow, prepare the body and console the bereaved, as is the African custom. The elderly women would go later to be with the family and assist with serving tea and bread to the mourners who would arrive to pay their last tribute.

At the Strong Yard in Roger Street, where Fuzani lived, there was a big open space. This was where the funeral service was conducted. The coffin was placed near a corner and seated beside it were Mrs Fuzani, all in black, and her children.

A large crowd was drawn to the funeral. Rugby players from the various teams in the Langa Rugby Football Union and cricketers from all over were dressed in their special kits. The officials came in their sports blazers.

While the service was on, the Busy Bee players took turns to pay respect by forming a guard of honour alongside the coffin. To have the funeral service conducted at home was not unusual, of course, because some Black families believed in having the service done there rather than at church. So the minister would be invited to come to the home of the bereaved.

Fuzani's funeral service was conducted by the minister of the Methodist church in Chapel Street.

Great words were said about this great hero, the most touching being a speech by one of the players, Michael Tsika, who started this way: "Let him rest, because he has been called by his ancestors.

"Let him rest, because he has joined his forefathers.

"Let him rest, because his body is tired.

"Lala ngoxolo, Cirha – Rest in peace, Cirha."

Cirha was Fuzani's clan name.

Tsika went on to explain how and when Fuzani started as captain of the team. He mentioned his commitment and the team's successes under his captainship, concluding with how the Fuzani Cup came into existence, and what it meant to the entire Busy Bee Rugby Club. Then he led the Busy Bee song: *"Yingwe emabalabala le Busy Bee"*, which sent tears running down Mrs Fuzani's cheeks.

Tsika continued, "The Fuzani family and the congregation at large, today we have come to bid farewell to a dedicated husband and father, a good sportsman, and a great hero. The speakers have painted to us who Fuzani really was, and we have no doubt that even those who were not close to him can understand and feel what a loss this is to our African community. Let us thank God for granting us the good days that we spent with this honourable gentleman. To Mrs Fuzani, thank you for being committed to the vow you made at the altar with this man: 'Until death do us part.' Weep no more because your husband did what he came to do on this earth – let him go and rest."

The Busy Bee players were the pall bearers. They carried the coffin to the waiting hearse outside the gate. The family were ushered into two cars and the rest of the people boarded the three buses which had been hired for the occasion.

All the other, visiting rugby players walked in front of the hearse, the Busy Bee players alongside. Everybody stood and watched the sad procession as it moved slowly down Stuckeris Street. When they reached Sir Lowry Road, all the players boarded the buses and the procession drove out to Woltemade cemetery in Maitland.

After the funeral, all the people went back to Fuzani's home to wash their hands and have a meal, as is the African custom.

My father dragged himself around the whole day. In the end, he decided to go to bed early.

He had lost a really good friend.

10

NYANGA WEST IS CREATED

One Saturday evening, at the beginning of 1960, two of our neighbours, Philemon Ngele and Solomon Mpazi, came to visit my father. Amongst other things, Ngele had come to repeat something that he had told Solomon earlier.

"Mbele, when last have you been to Langa? There's something that I picked up there, that raises a lot of concern."

"What is it, *madoda*? Gentlemen, you sound very serious," my father replied.

"*Hee*, Ngcelwane, *aqalile amaBhulu*. The *Boere* have started, and they're going to get us one by one," Solomon remarked.

"What are they doing this time?" my father said.

"Haven't you heard they're starting to move Black people from areas like Kensington, Elsies River and Retreat to a new location the other side of Langa?" Ngele explained.

"What's the name of the place, Sollie?" my father asked.

"I think it's called Nyanga West."

"Yes, it's Nyanga West!" Ngele confirmed.

"*Tyhini!* I know about that. I heard it from my son-in-law, Gcwanini. Do you recall that after he and Nombulelo were married, they moved from William Street to Retreat, that suburb on your way to Muizenberg? Well, they've moved again, to a tin-house location in Nyanga. Only on a temporary basis, though, because Gcwanini's boss told him he'd be moved to a new location eventually. The firm had been visited by inspectors from the Langa Administration Office and they wanted to know the names and addresses of all their Black employees. It seems the Administration Office is embarking on a forced removal of all Black people who do not live in locations," my father said.

"*He bethuna! Kuza kuthiwani?* What are we going to do?" Solomon said, very worried.

"There's nothing we can do right now, Sollie, except to wait and see."

"I also read in the newspaper that all Blacks who work in firms that fall under the Cape Town city council will be moved to this new location. And those working in areas like Bellville will be placed under the divisional council in Nyanga. This means that if this forced removal thing does happen, and comes to District Six, most of the residents of Cross Street will be moved to this place that you have just mentioned, what is it called again?"

"Nyanga West!" Sollie and Ngele chorused.

At this time Layton and I were attending school at Langa High. I was in Junior Certificate, Std 8, and my brother in Std 7. Some of our school mates from Kensington and Retreat were already moving to Nyanga West.

"Tata, some children at school are telling us that their families are moving to Nyanga West," Layton started one evening.

"Most of them are from Kensington and Retreat, Tata," I added.

"What about us, Tata? Are we also going to move?" Layton asked.

"*Khanithule!* Please shut up!" my mother screamed at us. "Can't you see your father doesn't want to talk about it?"

"*Hee, Mbele,* I had a visit from Bhayi this afternoon," she said one Tuesday evening soon afterwards while we were having supper.

"What, is he on holiday?" my father replied. "Or why did he come during the day?"

"No, he's out of work. You know how he always loses his jobs, but he's had it this time," my mother said, carefully putting down her fork.

My father stared at her and asked, "What do you mean?"

"He asked me to tell you that when he went to the Langa Office yesterday, his pass was stamped UPHUMAPHELE and he was given seven days to collect his belongings. He is going to be deported to Transkei."

"*Nkosi yam! Uza kuthini?* What is he going to do?" my father said, After a while he added, "I suppose the way he's been changing jobs, something like this was bound to happen. Poor Bhayi, what's he planning to do?"

"He says he's not going anywhere. He's planning to change his identity to 'Coloured'."

"Bhayi, man!" my father said, admiration in his voice.

"I just hope that he is serious because it's going to be very difficult for him to get another job without a valid pass."

"Does Tat'uBhayi have children, Tata?" Layton asked.

"*Hayi khona,* I don't think he's married," my father replied.

"*Hayi* shame," said Layton. "I feel very sorry for him."

"So do I," my mother added.

"Don't worry, and stop talking about it. Bhayi has his own way of doing things, I'm sure he will survive," my father said.

There was a lot of talk about the pending removal from District Six, but the implementation was disrupted by the 1960 Langa March.

THE 1960 LANGA MARCH

"Why are you back so early?" my mother asked, looking at the alarm clock which was showing half past eleven.

"Mama, we couldn't stay at school today. Something's happening at Langa. Most of the people didn't go to work. And the teachers told all the children who live outside Langa to go home," Layton burst out.

"Mama," I interrupted. "I've never seen so many people on the streets. At first I thought they were fighting, but later on I realised they were moving past our school towards the Langa flats. Some of the boys in my class that live in Langa said those people were all on strike."

"What are they striking for?" my mother asked, looking very surprised.

"Who knows? All I heard is that a lot of people have been turned back at the bus stops and at Langa station. Nobody was allowed to go to work today," Layton reported.

"That's strange! Your father never mentioned anything this morning and he has gone to work. In fact, everybody around here has gone to work, as usual."

"I suppose it's only happening in Langa. We didn't notice anything funny when we came up Hanover Street. Everything looked normal," Layton remarked.

My mother left us still talking about the Langa incident and told us that she was going to the butchery.

About twenty minutes later, she came back looking flushed.

"Hey, *bantwana bam*. You're right, my children. There's definitely something wrong and whatever you saw at Langa, has spread to District Six as well!" she said, quite out of breath.

Mama went to the window and called me. "Come and have a look, Nomvuyo. Look at those people running up Richmond Street. They're fleeing from a big crowd of Black men coming down Hanover Street towards the city, shouting, *'Izwe lethu, iAfrika.'* Even the shopkeepers have decided to close their shops. I was lucky to get to the butchery before the chaos."

My mother suddenly turned from the window. "Where's Layton?" She asked, looking worried.

"He's gone downstairs, Mama."

"Call him back, Nomvuyo, before he goes down Richmond Street. I don't want him to get into trouble."

"*Hey wena*, Layton! Come back! Mama wants you," I called through the window.

To my surprise, he turned back at once and ran back up the stairs.

This was the beginning of the Langa March of March 1960. After a few days some of the township residents who had friends and relatives in District Six decided to move in with their relatives while the pressure was on in the township.

It was awful to see some of them with black eyes and swollen arms, legs and knees from police intimidation. The poor fellows stayed indoors as much as possible, fearing to be caught or seen by the police. But the police were concentrating on the townships and tranquillity prevailed in District Six.

The Sunday gatherings at Cross Street continued, despite political tension. In fact, more people came because four township residents were now staying with relatives in our building. One of them, Peter Makupula, had lived at the Langa flats as a "bachelor" for some time because his wife and children were in the Eastern Cape. He was always smartly dressed, and so neat, it was hard to believe that he was not with his wife. His neatness and dress never went unnoticed because he had this one extraordinary feature: his complexion. He was very, very dark of skin.

"Allow me to confer this honour upon you," said Solomon to Peter, offering him the first glass from the bottle of beer. He added, joking, "What's wrong with you? You look absent-minded and darker than usual?"

"It's true, Bhut'Sollie. Absent-minded, yes. Darker, I don't know about that, but I'm worried about the clothes that I've left behind," replied Peter very seriously.

"But aren't they locked in a suitcase?"

"No, there was no time for that," Peter said miserably.

"Peter, why don't you make time after work and go and fetch your suitcase?" suggested Tatu'Benya.

"That's not possible. I can't expose myself to that type of harrassment and fear again." Turning to the others present, he said, "I don't think you realise how the residents got out of those flats during the raid."

"I've been telling him to do that for the past six days!" said Ernest Makupula, Peter's older brother, angered by his brother's stubborness.

"Steady now, Ernie, don't be so harsh with him," pleaded one of the elders. "He's not the only one who has some reservations about going back there. One old man from work has even decided to leave Cape Town for good. You know very well that it's not easy to take such a decision overnight, so please, don't blame your brother."

"I should think we must make sure the dust has settled before we can even think of sending our people back to Langa," suggested my father.

Just then, one of the neighbour's children came into the room to tell Peter there was somebody from Langa looking for him. Peter left the room immediately, but the conversation about the Langa flats continued.

"You must know that for most of the Langa flats residents it wasn't easy to escape the police," said one of the three visitors from Langa. "Some jumped from the top floor to the ground, using mattresses and sheets! Bullets were coming from all directions. Others were trying to get to the top floors because the police were already inside the buildings, moving from room to room, beating up everybody in their way. It was chaotic in the passages. The whole thing happened so fast, nobody knew exactly what was going on. We didn't know which direction to run to be safe. The safest thing we could think of doing was to try and get out of the flats and run to the bushes to hide."

"So you see why Peter is reluctant to go back?" added his friend from Langa, just as Peter walked in, followed by a stranger whom he introduced as his room-mate. The man had come to check on Peter, worried because he had not come back after the raid. He explained that Langa flats residents were checking on one another because quite a number of people had been arrested or shot at, and some had gone home, back to the country.

Another reason why he had come was to give Peter a duplicate key to their room. He had changed the door lock. The old one was broken when the police forced their way inside the room. Things were gradually returning to normal, he said, but soldiers had been deployed in the area and were watching the flats, day and night. Peter's clothes, apparently, were safe.

"I was worried about my friend, bhuti," the man said to Ernest, Peter's brother. "I know that he has a problem with White policemen because of the colour of his skin. They probably think that he is a communist from Central Africa," he said, and they all laughed.

My father was very concerned about my eldest sister Nombulelo who stayed in Nyanga then. She had just had her third child, and her husband was hiding somewhere as word had gone round that there were collaboraters whose faces had been covered with hoods during the strike, and who had identified the leaders of the strike. A lot of innocent people were put into custody in this exercise.

My brother-in-law Gcwanini visited us three days later, and he was clearly worried. He had last seen his wife a week before and had kept wondering how he was going to get through to her. He was tired and edgy and I felt very sorry for him. He was relieved when my father suggested that Layton should go to Nombulelo and the children and stay with them for as long as things were unsettled.

After supper, Gcwanini, who had been hiding in William Street, told us of different incidents involving strikers who were hiding from the police.

"Tata, you remember Skhoma, my friend, the one you used to call 'Makhuluskop' because of his big head?" he began.

"Oh yes, I remember him. Where's he staying now?"

"At Nyanga, Tata."

"What about him?"

"I met him in town yesterday. Did he make me laugh, the way he talked about how he was picked up!"

"I'm sure his head looked even bigger," my father said.

This made his son-in-law burst into laughter before he continued. "'Gcwanini!' he said to me with big eyes, '*AmaBhulu andiba-mba, mfondini!*' – The *Boere* arrested me, man!

"'Where, Skhoma?' I asked.

"'At home. I was in the kitchen when I heard the sound of a vehicle screeching to a halt. I looked through the window. *Mfondini!* There was a saracen stopping right in front of my house.'

"'Yho! What did you do?' I asked.

"'I ran out of the kitchen and hid under a bed. Gcwanini! Shock can make you do funny things. You know what? The bed had no mattress and I didn't even realise that. The mattress was standing outside in the yard, being aired for the day.'"

"'Ha! ha! Then what, Skhoma?' I asked.

"'Don't worry, Gcwanini, I was lucky. Those hooded *mpimpis* could not idenfity me as one of the leaders of the strike and I was released on the same day.'"

"He was really very lucky," my father agreed. "If you go in, you usually don't come out."

"*Kanti,* Tata. But Tata, one old man, also from Nyanga, was just as lucky," Gcwanini continued. "He ran out of the house to the forest. I suppose he didn't know that all the townships were surrounded by soldiers. Inside the forest, he came across soldiers with guns ..."

"Didn't they shoot him and bury him right there?" my father asked.

"No, Tata. He was so shocked that he dropped down and lost consciousness!"

"Poor thing!"

"He was lucky because they were young soldiers, just out of school, who felt sorry for him. They aren't as cruel as the the older guys, you know. They gave him first aid and when he revived, they told him to go home."

"They must have considered his age," my father suggested.

The days passed. The Black residents of District Six heard about more disturbing incidents in the townships. The people from Langa who had taken refuge in District Six were invited to stay until the situation calmed down.

What had been happening was also a huge story in the newspapers. According to the press, the police network had "cleaned up" the townships. On the 7th of April, 1 500 people were arrested. The strike, which had started on the 21st of March when 6 000 men gathered at the bachelor quarters in Langa to march to the police station, was broken, it was reported.

Although District Six was close by the route they took, none of us had joined in the big march three days later. My father read to us from the newspaper how people had spontaneously gathered in Nyanga and Langa and marched all the way to the centre of town. Thirty thousand Black people marched, twelve abreast, over De Waal Drive to the police station at Caledon Square.

It was a miracle that only two people lost their lives in the unrest.

The event had completely disrupted our school programme. Langa High School, unfortunately, was not far from the Langa flats, and the entire area was very tense. On the day after the march, we learnt in District Six that one of the classrooms had been burned down.

While we were standing in groups in the school yard, just before assembly on the morning of the 21st of March, we heard a loud scream coming from the left wing of the school building, followed by crying.

"Did you hear that? Where did it come from?" I whispered, nervously.

"From one of the Std 10 classrooms," my friend, Gwen, whispered back.

We all ran in that direction. Somebody was crying alright. It was Nosiba, a Std 10 pupil, holding the remains of her satchel.

"I've lost all my books!" she sobbed.

Some teachers had come rushing out to find out what was amiss.

"It's Nosiba, *mfundisi,* and she's lost all her books," we reported.

Nosiba was by now hysterical, and was taken by one of the teachers to the Domestic Science room, where she was given a glass of water to drink. The rest of us were sent home.

It was not until a month later that school returned to normal. We had fallen behind schedule and were told that we would have to catch up for the mid-year exams.

"Some of the classes will have to attend school on Saturday as well," the principal announced. "There's too much catching up to be done."

Later on we realised that he was referring to the two classes who had to write external examinations, Stds 8 and 10.

Some of our male classmates at Langa High School had also been arrested. I still remember how we used to whisper about it during break time, wondering if they would be back for the mid-year examinations.

LEAVING HOME AND RETURNING

After passing Std 8 in 1960, I decided to go for teacher training. This of course was going to dig deep into my father's pocket because there were no teachers' training colleges for African students in Cape Town at the time, and this meant that I had to go to a boarding school in the Eastern Cape.

"I don't mind paying, Nomvuyo, and I also think you'll make a good teacher," my father said. "But will you feel alright away from us?"

"Oh, Tata, a big girl like me? There are much younger children who are at boarding school. I'll be okay," I said, full of confidence.

For the next two years I attended a college near King William's Town. After the first six months, I came back for teaching practice. I thought of the Chapel Street school that I attended for my first years of schooling and decided to go and see the principal.

On the first Monday of my June vacation I walked down to Chapel Street. It was about eight o'clock in the morning. When I approached the building, the pupils were still outside. Class had not yet started. When I was about three yards away, a boy came out of the gate with a bell in his hand. He started ringing it.

Oh! They do have a bell now, I thought to myself. Some progress at last, remembering how we had to be called back to class.

But the school was still using the church hall, I noticed. I waited outside to give them time for their morning assembly. I could hear Miss Thutha's voice from outside.

One of the pupils saw me and I suppose he must have told the principal there was somebody at the door, because a few minutes later, one of the bigger pupils came and asked me in.

Hayibo! The place had not changed a bit! All the pupils stood up to show respect when I walked in, just like we used to do in the old days. But I noticed that the pupils were fewer in number.

There was my former principal, Mr Kakaza, much, much older than the last time I had seen him. What a warm welcome I received! It was even announced to the pupils that I was a product of the school, and I had to show them where I used to sit in the Std 2 class.

There was no change at the school save for the bell and the new school furniture. Miss Thutha, my Sub A teacher, was so excited that she hugged and kissed me.

128

Because there were no teachers' training colleges for Black students in the Western Cape at the time, I (front, 2nd from right) had to leave home in 1960 to attend a college near King William's Town. I was fortunate, however, to do my practical teaching at my old primary school in Chapel Street in District Six.

"I'm still training, okay? Not a qualified teacher," I said to her.

"Don't be so bashful, you will be," she said with a big smile on her face. "I'm so proud of you!"

I enjoyed every minute of my teaching practice.

I was allowed to teach Stds 1 and 2, much to my disappointment, my favourite class then already being Sub A. But I decided to make the most of it. I was going to impress my two teachers. Also, I was going to help the children and boost my image, for I knew most of the children's families.

"Are you our new teacher, miss?" a little one asked me.

"For the time being, class."

"We'd love to have you as our teacher."

"Why?"

"You're young and you've already taught us a few interesting new things."

"I'll be with you for three weeks only, so we'd better make the most of it," I said.

I got on very well with my classes and my father and mother were getting positive remarks from the children's parents about their "new teacher". Two of my pupils lived in Cross Street.

"Nomvuyo, you're doing very well, my child," my father remarked.

"I'm also excited about it, Tata," I said. "Thank you for sending me to college."

LEAVING NO. 22 FOR GOOD

In August of 1963, my father received a letter asking him to report at the Drill Hall in connection with arrangements that had been made by the Local Authorities for him and his family. We had been expecting it, of course, because some of the Black Cross Street residents had already received their notices.

My father went to the Drill Hall on the date indicated and returned with the news that we were to be moved to Nyanga West. The Coloureds could still stay in District Six, but the law could not allow us Blacks to stay there any longer. It was made that simple.

"How did it go, Mbele?" my mother started later that evening.

My brother jumped at the opportunity and added, "Did you ask them any questions, Tata?"

We had meant to ask my father about the interview since he had returned from there, but my mother kept on saying, "Not now, can't you see that he's still reading his paper? I don't want to disturb him."

"You have no idea how we feel, Mama," I said. "We're dying of curiosity."

"Give me time, I'll ask him after supper," she said.

"UMama! You like to shelve important things for later."

"I'll let you do it then."

"Sorry, Mama, I'll wait," I apologised.

My father's reply was short and to the point. "Do you think that the *Boere* will ever give a Black person a chance to argue about what they have already decided?"

I knew how my father resented the idea of staying in a location, and could understand how he was feeling at that point.

The residents talked about nothing else but the forced removals. Even the Coloured neighbours were concerned, because we had stayed together and shared so much for so many years.

"I can think of nothing else," Auntie Susie said to my mother one day. "The Whites really think they can throw people around!"

Some of them even suggested that the Blacks resist the removal. Nobody took heed of the suggestion because the Langa March and its consequences were still vivid in the people's minds. The main concern was the fact that letters were sent only to those people who were staying with their families. All our bachelor neighbours did not receive a word. They were supposed to be staying at the bachelor quarters in Langa, so they were just being ignored. What was going to happen to them?

The removal was going to bring a lot of change to people's lives: for immediate neighbours, there was no guarantee that they would be living together as neighbours in Nyanga West. The fear was that we would be scattered all over. To those who walked to their place of work, it meant budgeting for bus or train fares in the future.

To the children, it meant making new friends and attending new schools. And what was going to happen to the Chapel Street school that held such indelible memories for the Black children of District Six?

To housewives, it meant cutting down on grocery lists because the increase in rent and fares to work – with no increase in people's wages – left less money for food.

To the worshippers it meant travelling long distances to get to church. To everybody, it meant paying higher rent, adjusting to the conditions of Nyanga West, and changing their social life style.

We started packing our stuff into boxes. As a qualified teacher, I was then teaching at a primary school in Nyanga, but I was still staying at home and helping with the chores and grocery bills.

The shop owners in Hanover Street assisted us a lot by offering empty boxes.

During the third week of September, we were advised of our new address and the date of our removal: on the 4th of October we were to expect the removal lorry, some time after 9 o'clock in the morning, which was to take us to NY 75 No. 7 Section 2, Nyanga West. The rent was going to be eight rand and five cents, payable by the 7th of each month.

"What a big difference! From one rand ten cents to eight rand five cents!" Layton said, looking at the new rent card.

"Put that away, *wena*, you, before Tata sees you!" I warned.

"Don't be silly, *kwedini*! Put that card back where you found it!" my mother scolded.

"Okay, okay. Why is everybody's nerves so on edge these days?" my brother said, putting the rent card back inside the wardrobe.

"You'll know why, when you won't be able to go to the movies on Saturday any more," I assured him.

"I won't mind, because there are no movies in the location, anyway," he said, though I knew that deep down he did not mean a word of what he was saying. Going to the movies on Saturdays was one of his week's highlights. The removal was really creating a lot of tension.

At about ten o'clock on the 4th of October, a big lorry stopped in front of our building and the driver asked for my father. My father was at work in Observatory, so my mother had to attend to the man. He gave her the key to our new home and they started loading the boxes on to the truck. I was worried about the furniture because it had to be moved down the flight of stairs with its thirteen steps, and it was obvious that the people doing the job were not skilled in their work.

"Mind those boxes, there are dishes inside," my mother warned as one man tried to lift a box.

"Mama, *andibaqondi aba bantu* – I don't have confidence in these people. Can you see how clumsy they are?" I whispered.

"Alright, Marge, I'll help with the boxes of crockery," said our old friend Neville who had specially come to assist us with the move.

"Steady!" someone shouted as the men were struggling to get the wardrobe down the stairs.

Some of the Coloured neighbours helped us get the furniture on the lorry.

"Nomvuyo, please go upstairs and check if everything has been taken out!" my mother asked me when everything was more or less gone.

The room was empty and looked much bigger than before. It was very neat because my mother had even washed the walls. I took a last long look at it. To think that I had spent twenty years of my life in this room!

I moved over to the window to take a last glimpse of the view that I used to enjoy so much, the yellow Muir Street Zainatul Mosque, the harbour, the sea at a distance, looking very calm in the fine weather. I could feel the emptiness inside me. Quickly I moved from the window, stopping at the door. The room was full of light because there were no curtains at the windows, and the walls were sparkling at the sun's reflection. I remembered how cosy it used to be in winter.

Now I was forced to get out, simply because I was African. I wanted to cry. I quickly shut the door and ran downstairs.

This was the saddest moment of our lives, having to say goodbye to our neighbours. They all came to bid us farewell.

My mother was standing with Aunt Susie, Esme and Mrs Morris.

"How far is this location from here?" Esme asked.

"It's quite far. From Sir Lowry Road you have to take a bus to Claremont, then another one to Nyanga West."

"It's far," Esme agreed. "It means we'll never see you again."

"I suppose so," my mother said sadly.

I looked at her but she avoided my eyes. I could see she was about to cry. I turned my head and talked to Neville and my brother.

"Thanks for your help, Neville," Layton was saying.

"It's for the good times, pal!" Neville said, shaking my brother's hand and then hugging me.

The older Coloured men were helping the driver tie a thick rope right round the load.

"It's tight now, it's going to be okay," one of the neighbours assured the driver, who thanked them and got on to the lorry.

When the engine of the lorry started running, Auntie Susie said to my mother, "We meet to part and we part to meet. Go well!"

My mother and I scrambled into the lorry. Layton was going by bus. I sat squeezed in next to the window, waving at my friends as the lorry slowly moved down Richmond Street. With tears in my eyes I took a last glimpse at No. 22 Cross Street as we turned into Stuckeris Street.

"*Sala kahle,* District Six," I whispered.

Thirty-three years later, an article appeared in the *Cape Argus* of 5 August 1996 under the heading, "District Six Blacks Urged to Submit Claims". The article started as follows: "Perceptions that District Six had been inhabited exclusively by Coloured people were inaccurate ... ."

They were. Few outsiders knew about our lives there. I hope that through this book people now will get to know more of the truth about District Six.

LIST OF BLACK FAMILIES WHO LIVED IN DISTRICT SIX

Name of street	*Surnames*
Adam	Mabilwana, Gxelesha, Ngcozana
Albertus	Mdlalana
Ashley	Mandindi, Mahlangeni, Ncapai, Tulumane
Ayre	Mkhutshulwa, Soloshe, Sidinana, Ncube
Caledon	Nkqayi, Mandondo, Mantsha, Mgudlwa, Madikane, Sihlahla, Shosha, Simani
Chapel	Gcilishe, Xakana, Ngxabi, Mbokomo, Mabusela
Clifton	Qusheka, Mqela
Combrinck	Hakula, Madlingozi
Commercial	Nwele
Constitution	Mgutyungwa, Mayeye, Nkungwana, Ndabambi, Kambi, Skheweza
Cross	Ngele, Makupula, Benya, Guzana, Ngcelwane, Njobe, Dayile, Mabandla, Makhasi, Mpazi, Nkanjeni, Makhabane, Mfaco, Ntshiba, Mahanjana
De Villiers	Tibini, Pepetha, Vanda, Makupula, Nqwata, Luningo, Memani
Gore	Manjingolo, Dunjwa
Hanover	Canda, Mguncula, Vanda, Ncanywa, Mnguni, Khumalo, Jodwana, Sitshetshe, Marubelela, Sigabi, Nodada, Maqhina, Gqotso, Xotongo, Gqasana, Mapukata
Harrington	Mrwebi, Masiza, Ngwanya
Horstley	Guzana, Ngaba
Kent	Conjwa, Mrubata, Siga, Madalane
Longmarket	Xayiya, Mavumbe, Ncapai, Ndiki, Skenjane
Maud Lane	Majokweni

McGregor	Mdleleni
McKenzie	Ntethe, Vellem
Mount	Hokolo, Tshongoyi, Honono, Bala
Primrose	Bokwana
Reform	Qaba, Tukulu, Plaatjie, Guwa, Ndawo, Zantsi
Rogers	Ncevu, Tsika, Maliwa, Fuzani, Luthuli
Roos	Mbenyane, Plaatjie, Mgudlwa
Sackville	Mbunye, Selani
Selkirk	Ntontela, Masiza, Mabusela, Majikela, Mankoma
Stone	Mqolo, Mtshibe, Bungane, Mdlalo, Gush, Ndunge Mbingeleli, Yamba
Stuckeris	Cakwe, Mhlauli, Mkonto, Mafongozi, Lugalo, Ngabase, Dywili, Msuthu, Mpofu
Tennant	Makoko, Ndiki
Thomas	Mlombo, Mketo, Stemela
Tyne	Tena, Khwatshube, Kobi, Nko, Mokoeng, Pau, Seti
Van der Leur	Sogiba, Myataza, Limba, Jeku, Maqula
Virginia	Qengwa, Mkhulisi
Wicht	Betela, Kondile, Kuse, Ndzabela, Masiba, Matshotyana
William	Cele, Ngele, Ngomela, Nogoduka, Bunyula, Malobola, Gontsana, Mvumvu, Mshumpela, Nokhubeka

WORD LIST

amaBhele – the Mbele clan
amaBhulu – the Boere, Afrikaners; sometimes: police
amakhosi – jailbirds
amper baas – literally: almost boss
babie – Muslim shopkeeper
basella/pasella – free gift with a purchase
bhuti – brother; term of respect for another man
ewe – yes
fish oil – cooking oil
Hayibo! – exclamation of surprise
Hayi khona! – Oh no!
Hey wena! – Hey you!
ibhunga – disciplinary committee
induna – supervisor
izwe lethu, iAfrika – our land, Africa
lobola – cattle given to bride's father to seal wedding agreement
madoda – gentlemen
mama – mother; term of respect for a married woman
mafikizolo – newcomer
manene – gentlemen
maskanda – pianist
mfondini – man; term used instead of a contemporary's name
mfundisi – teacher
mpimpi – collaborator; police informer
muti – herbs
Nkosi yam – my Lord
Sala kahle – Stay well
sangoma – traditional African healer
sisi – sister; sometimes a pet name for a little girl
siyakudla – charging you
skollie – gangster
slim – clever
Suka wena! – Go away!
tata – father; term of respect for a married man
Tat'u... – indicating a clan name
Thiza! – exclamation of surprise, or shock
tsotsi – gangster
Tyhini! – exclamation of disbelief
ukutrokwa – being deported
umgalelo – stokvel, a club for pooling of funds and mutual support,
    usually organised in rotation at members' homes
umkhwelo – house party
uphumaphele – sending back to the homelands
xhwele – traditional healer; sangoma